Her Ladyship's Guide to

the Art of Conversation

For Kit,

whose conversational skills need no assistance from me

First published in the United Kingdom in 2016 by

Batsford

1 Gower Street

London

WC1E 6HD

An imprint of Pavilion Books Company Ltd

ISBN: 9781849943451

A CIP catalogue record for this book is available from the British Library.

20 19 18 17 16
10 9 8 7 6 5 4 3 2 1

Reproduction by Mission Productions, Hong Kong
Printed by Toppan Leefung Printing Ltd, China

This book can be ordered direct from the publisher at the website
www.pavilionbooks.com, or try your local bookshop.

Her Ladyship's Guide to
the Art of Conversation

Caroline Taggart

BATSFORD

Contents

99

"

Introduction

LIZA [to Freddy, who is in convulsions
of suppressed laughter]:
Here! what are you sniggering at?
FREDDY: The new small talk.
You do it so awfully well.
LIZA: If I was doing it proper,
what was you laughing at?

George Bernard Shaw

"

I n a famous scene from Shaw's 1913 play *Pygmalion*, the inspiration
for the musical *My Fair Lady*, the Cockney flower-girl Eliza is making
her first foray into 'polite society' and trying to pass herself off as a
'lady'. Her mentor, Professor Higgins, has given her strict instructions on
what to talk about: 'The weather and everybody's health'. He intends her
to stick to 'Fine day' and 'How do you do'. Eliza, however, adheres to the
letter rather than the spirit of his advice: she manages to tell a shocked
upper-class tea party about a gin-addicted aunt who allegedly died of
influenza, but whom she believes was murdered by 'them she lived with'
for the sake of a straw hat.

This was in the time when the art of conversation was part of every young
lady and gentleman's education. So if it could go so disastrously wrong
when etiquette was widely understood and firmly enforced, how much
more difficult is it now that we are generally left to muddle through as
best we can?

More recently, a friend of Her Ladyship's reported her bitter
experiences of the sort of dinner party organised to help single people
meet one another. Time after time she had found it impossible to draw
her companions out, despite the fact that they had come deliberately
in order to meet people like her. What should have been harmless
conversational openings ('What do you do?', 'Where do you come from?')
turned into something like an interrogation, because the responses were
so brief and weren't followed by, 'And what about you?' 'It makes you
realise why some of these people can't get partners,' she said between
gritted teeth. 'They just don't know the rules.'

So what, in today's easy-going society, are the rules?

Perhaps the best way to begin is by considering what conversation
is – and what it is not. A friend of Her Ladyship's remembers fondly
a snippet she overheard in her student days: two Oxford dons were
crossing a college quadrangle and one was heard to say firmly to the
other, 'And nineteenthly …'

Her Ladyship confesses to considerable admiration for anyone who can follow a train of thought so clearly that they can keep tabs on nineteen points of it. But, she ventures to suggest, these two academics were not having a conversation. One, despite the informal setting, was delivering a lecture; the other was listening either meekly or with growing indignation and almost certainly waiting for his companion to pause for breath so that he could edge a word in.

> **66**
>
> **Conversation, Her Ladyship believes, is like a game in which the ball is batted around among the participants: not rigidly back and forth, back and forth, as in tennis, but in a more relaxed, beach-volleyball style.**
>
> **99**

Another friend reflected on a 'conversation' he once had at a party with a woman who talked entirely about herself. Her activities, her holidays, her plans for moving house – whatever she had to say, she was at the centre of it. 'I don't like this woman,' Her Ladyship's friend thought, 'because she clearly has no interest in me.' That woman wasn't having a conversation either.

From those two negative examples, we can move on to a positive one, summed up by Dr Johnson's maxim that 'the happiest conversation' is one where there is 'no competition, no vanity, but a calm, quiet interchange of sentiments'. It's an invitation to someone else to engage with you, and an opportunity for you to engage with them. Conversation, Her Ladyship believes, is like a game in which the ball is batted around among the participants: not rigidly back and forth, back and forth, as in tennis, but in a more relaxed, beach-volleyball style. Everyone puts a hand on the ball when it comes their way, contributing their bit when they are in the best position to do so. No one hogs the ball – the rules of the game don't permit it. But no one is entirely left out either. Good players – and good conversationalists – seem to know instinctively how to pass, making it easy for others to take over. Weaker players may fumble or drop the ball, or hit it in an odd direction so that someone else has to go out of their way to retrieve it. This can be annoying or embarrassing, so it's important to keep the ball in play. Finally, and to revert to the 'it's not like tennis' analogy, there is no place in this game for aces, smashes or double faults.

> **"**
> **It has often been said – not least by Her Ladyship – that the essence of good manners is to make the other person feel comfortable.**
> **"**

But even if we basically understand these 'rules', the truth is that most of us hate the idea of walking into a room full of strangers, all of whom seem to know each other. It's worst if we are on our own, but even if we're not, it seems cowardly – and somehow wrong – to spend the entire evening talking to a partner or colleague. Yet whether we are on our own or part of a couple, it is often difficult to strike up conversations with people we have never met before. We don't know what to say or how to say it and we can't believe that anyone is going to care anyway. But there are tricks and techniques we can learn that will turn a potential ordeal into a source of enjoyment or even, in a business context, profit.

Conversation isn't – or shouldn't be – a painful duty or an albatross around anyone's neck. It isn't a test in which you pass or fail, achieve distinction or just scrape through. It can be about anything from Bach to Brussels sprouts, photography to the Periodic Table, and it's a potentially joyous, life-enriching experience. Most of this book will be about social conversation – the kind you have with a stranger at a party – but it will also take in dos and don'ts of work conversation and a few tips on dating.

It has often been said – not least by Her Ladyship – that the essence of good manners is to make the other person feel comfortable. If so, then the essence of good conversation is to make the other person feel interesting. But it helps if you can make yourself sound interesting too. How to achieve these two objectives is the purpose of this book.

If the very idea has you squirming in your chair with embarrassment, please read on.

"

Before You Say a Word

From the moment I saw you I distrusted you. I felt that you were false and deceitful. I am never deceived in such matters. My first impressions of people are invariably right.

Oscar Wilde

I t is said that most people will form an opinion of you within the first moments of meeting you. Some experts say this happens within as little as 30 seconds, others as much as two minutes. It doesn't matter. The point is that, once the opinion is formed, it isn't easy to make anyone change their minds. That first impression really is all-important. So how do you make it as positive as possible?

Let's imagine you are going to a party where you are worried you will know very few people. It will help, of course, to be confident that you look your best. While it is always wrong to be overdressed, Her Ladyship assumes that you weren't planning to wear an evening gown and diamond necklace to a midweek supper party. For most day-to-day occasions – and particularly if no dress code is specified – you can't go far wrong with 'smart casual'. If you know you look good in that little black dress or are more assured in a jacket and tie than an open-necked shirt, wear them. If you're going to a private party, it may be wise to 'mirror' what your host and hostess are likely to be doing: if you know they tend to dress up a bit, do the same; if they are jeans-and-jumper people, it's probably best not to wear a suit (unless you are coming straight from work, in which case you might make a point of taking your tie off the moment you come in the door). If you're really worried, ring your host in advance and ask. But the most important advice – particularly if you are anxious about attending an event alone – is to wear something in which you feel self-assured and comfortable. This is not the time to try out that recent purchase that you suspect in your heart of hearts was a mistake.

When you get there

In the room where you leave your coat, or in the bathroom, give yourself a quick once-over before joining the mêlée. Obviously if facilities are limited you shouldn't hog them, but it is worth taking a moment to spruce yourself up.

Check your hair, your make-up and your clothes. Make sure zips are done up and underwear is suitably covered. Examine the effect of any buttons you mean to leave undone: if in doubt, err on the side of caution and do one of them up. Stand up straight, chin up, shoulders back and stomach in – all those things you were told in gym or Pilates classes come into their own at a time like this. You aren't aiming for parade ground precision – that can be as off-putting as a slouch. You just want to look smart in a way that has nothing to do with dress; it will help you look confident and that should make you feel more confident too.

Take a couple of deep breaths, as if you were diving into a swimming pool, and plunge in.

66

Check your hair, your make-up and your clothes ... You just want to look smart in a way that has nothing to do with dress; it will help you look confident and that should make you feel more confident too.

99

Once you are in the party room, don't give your appearance another thought. Easier said than done, of course, but Her Ladyship assures you that fiddling with necklaces, hemlines or hair will make you look either nervous or flirtatious, at least one of which is not the effect you are aiming for.

The subject of introductions and introducing yourself will be dealt with in Chapter 3. For the moment, let us focus on the non-verbal aspects of your approach to others.

Smile

If you enter a room shrinkingly, as if you would prefer to remain unobtrusively in a corner, people are less likely to take notice of you than if you are wearing a confident smile (whatever inner turmoil it may be masking). If you can make yourself seem self-assured, strangers will think you are more interesting than if you appear to be apologising for daring to be in the same room as them. Or, to put it more bluntly, if you give the impression that you aren't very interesting, people will believe you and steer clear.

> **66**
>
> **If you do shake hands, do it as if you mean it ... The happy medium involves gentle but noticeable pressure.**
>
> **99**

Shaking hands

It is rarely wrong to shake hands when you are introduced to someone for the first time, or when you encounter a business acquaintance. This assumes, however, that the other person doesn't have a glass in one hand and a sausage roll in the other, or isn't covered in charcoal from the barbecue. If it is obvious that a handshake would be inconvenient, a smile, a nod and a conventional greeting such as 'How nice to meet you/see you again' are perfectly acceptable. 'How do you do?' (to which the only correct answer is 'How do you do?') is becoming a little old-fashioned and should be reserved for formal occasions or when you are meeting someone who is likely to expect formality.

If you do shake hands, do it as if you mean it. Her Ladyship has a deep aversion to those people (and it is a common fault among women of a certain age and style) who lay their hand limply in someone else's, as if the effort of even the slightest squeeze would require them to send for their smelling salts. At the other end of the scale, however, she would prefer neither to be crushed by someone who has modelled his approach on Arnold Schwarzenegger, nor to have her hand pumped vigorously up and down by someone who seems to think he will fill a bucket of water if he keeps going long enough. The happy medium involves gentle but noticeable pressure. Never offer your hand to be kissed unless you are of a rank that entitles you to wear a tiara or are being deliberately flirtatious with someone who will respond in kind.

When you shake hands, smile and briefly make eye contact. Don't stare hard into the other person's eyes unless you want to be taken for a Mafioso confirming an understanding about your next hit.

Most people would say that anything more affectionate than a handshake is inappropriate when meeting someone for the first time. Kissing on one or both cheeks in these circumstances is the preserve of the very young, clubbing set, while hugging – to the reserved British, at least – is too intimate until you know someone well. As always, however, there are exceptions to the rule: if you can in all sincerity say to someone, 'I'm so glad to meet you at last – I feel I know you already', you may choose to accompany this with a hug. But be guided by the other person: if you sense that this sort of effusion would embarrass them, hold back. And for maximum avoidance of embarrassment, never, ever offer to hug a teenage boy (especially if you are a teenage girl) unless he makes the first move.

Body language

Little things like the tilt of your head or shoulder can give away your feelings, making you look uncomfortable, critical, quizzical… You may not be aware of them, but they contribute to the impression others will have of you.

"

Body language signals

Here are some of the most commonly observed 'signals' that you may give off unconsciously:

• Folding your arms suggests you're closed in, unapproachable. Open them a little and people will realise that you are 'receiving' them and open to conversation.

• Clutching your handbag in front of you makes you look nervous – are you expecting someone to steal it? In fact, any gesture that involves holding an arm, a glass or anything else between you and the person you are talking to looks as if you are protecting yourself from an unspecified attack.

• Don't stand with your hands in your pockets: in addition to being slovenly, it makes you look bored.

• Standing with your legs apart can also give off aggressive vibes. No one is suggesting that you stand to attention, military style, but reasonably upright, with the feet no more than hip-width apart and the weight evenly balanced on both feet, is the smartest stance. Remember, you are thinking about first impressions: once those crucial moments have passed, you can afford to be more relaxed.

• Leaning away from someone suggests you're uncomfortable with what they are saying, that you aren't interested in their overtures or that they are invading your personal space.

"

> • On the other hand, if you are sitting down, leaning slightly towards someone makes you look interested and engaged with what they are saying.
>
> • Holding your head up gives an impression of confidence and alertness, but can easily be overdone: if you hold it too high you will seem to be 'looking down your nose' at people, while sticking your chin out can be interpreted as aggressive or defiant (unfortunate if you happen to have a long chin and nowhere else to put it, but worth bearing in mind nevertheless).

Unless the room is very crowded and you have no alternative, don't stand too close to someone you don't know well. As a rule of thumb, about a metre apart is comfortable for most non-intimates. You both have to reach out in order to shake hands, and are too far apart for anything more affectionate – which is as it should be. If you are crushed against someone you don't know, make a joke of it and take the opportunity to introduce yourself: 'This is cosy, isn't it? I'm … and it's lovely to meet you. I'd shake hands but I don't think I can move mine.' This should break the ice and may even enable one of you to suggest you move to another, less crowded part of the room so that you can talk.

Then there is the question of facial expression. How many times in a trashy novel have you read of the villain, 'His smile didn't reach his eyes'? Make sure yours does. One communications expert offers this tip for conveying enthusiasm when greeting a stranger: imagine that you have just spotted an old friend, someone for whom you feel great fondness but whom you haven't seen for a long time. Your eyes will light up; apparently even your eyebrows will soften. Both you and your new acquaintance will be delighted.

On the other hand, don't attempt to hold a smile for longer than feels natural. Once the corners of your mouth start to tighten and your teeth begin to grit, you can be sure that the ecstatic look will have left your eyes and your whole demeanour will be artificial. Relax and listen to what the other person is saying – if you can respond with warmth, you'll be able to smile naturally again.

Eye contact

Everyone knows that avoiding eye contact makes you look shifty or at best unfriendly. Think about how you feel when your doctor stares at her computer screen throughout your consultation, as opposed to when she turns and looks at you. Think also how off-putting it is trying to talk to someone wearing mirrored sunglasses. You feel you can't communicate because you can't see their eyes.

Eye contact is important, but it has to be carefully managed.

Eye contact is important, but it has to be carefully managed. If you hold it for more than a few seconds, it can appear aggressive; but if you glance away when someone is talking to you it looks as if your mind has wandered. Try looking the person in the eye, then looking at their mouth and then back at their eyes. Give an occasional encouraging nod to show that you are paying attention and are interested.

If you are doing the talking, break eye contact every few seconds and flick your eyes to one side or towards the ceiling. This will make it look as if you are gathering your thoughts and intend to carry on. If you look down, it will look as if you have finished what you are saying and encourage the other person to leap in. This may sound very technical, but Her Ladyship assures you that it is not. If you take note of how you behave when you are chatting comfortably to a friend, you'll probably realise you both do it automatically.

If you want to attract the attention of someone on the other side of the room, catch their eye and smile; perhaps raise your hand slightly in a low-key greeting (by 'slightly' Her Ladyship means not much above shoulder height – you are saying hello, not asking permission to leave the room). If they return the look, the smile or the wave, you can feel free to approach them: they would look away if they didn't want to know. Don't stare: that is not only rude, it can make you seem either threatening or a little crazy, or both. And bear in mind that prolonged eye contact produces a hormonal reaction that brings with it sexual overtones. Perfectly OK if you mean it; less good if you don't.

All that being said, body language is not an exact science. The person you are talking to could be scratching her nose because it is itchy, not because she is trying to disguise the fact that she is telling a lie. Don't obsess about any of this, but if you think you are bad at it, and making that good first impression really matters, practise. Practise in front of a mirror, or an 'audience' of a friend or two; if you're obliged to do a lot of socialising or public speaking and are nervous about it, seek help from a professional communications expert.

Be Prepared

'I certainly have not the talent which some people possess,' said Darcy, 'of conversing easily with those I have never seen before ...' 'My fingers,' said Elizabeth, 'do not move over this instrument in the masterly manner which I see so many women's do ... But then I have always supposed it to be my own fault – because I would not take the trouble of practising.'

Jane Austen

"

I n an ideal world, the host of any party will introduce fellow guests to each other with a brief explanation of who they both are (there'll be more on that in the next chapter). Unfortunately there will be occasions when your host has vanished and you are left to your own devices. Whatever the circumstances, when you're meeting new people, someone is bound to ask you what you do, how you know the host or (if you happen to be meeting a royal) if you have come far. If you want to be sure of having interesting responses to these questions, it's as well to give them some thought in advance.

Her Ladyship should mention here that it used to be considered impolite to ask someone what they did. It was seen either as a covert way of sizing up how much someone might be worth; or as something of an insult, because it assumed that they had to demean themselves by working for a living. That particular taboo has largely gone out of fashion, but still holds good if you are talking to someone with a title: while some aristocrats have made names for themselves as furniture designers or racing correspondents, many find that running their estates and the other obligations of noblesse take up most of their time – but may find it difficult to say so without sounding conceited.

The obvious questions

Before you arrive at any social gathering, think up answers that are likely to be interesting to another person and to stimulate further conversation. 'I'm just a civil servant – a bit boring, really' (a real-life reply once given in Her Ladyship's hearing) is a killer. A modicum of forethought would have enabled that man to say, perhaps, 'I'm just a civil servant, but I leave at five o'clock and get to work on the garden, which is my real love.' This would have given the conversation a positive turn while downplaying the fact that he didn't want to talk about work. Another option would have been to throw the ball back into the other person's

" "

And what do you do?

I work for the government and I'm not allowed to talk about it.

Awkward silence. 'Oh, are you a spy?' is probably inappropriate. So, how about:

And what do you do?

I work for the government and I'm not allowed to talk about it.

So what are you allowed to talk about? The weather? Or shall I tell you about me?

Sarcastic, but if you say it brightly enough you might get away with it. Better, surely, if your newfound spy friend has an answer prepared:

I work for the government, but I'd rather talk about you.

A bit flirtatious? Then consider:

I work for the government, but it's a bit technical – I don't want to bore you. Do you go to the theatre at all? That's one of my great loves.

If you do enjoy the theatre, all is well. If not, counter with your preference for the cinema or concerts or the outdoors – there's no harm in a little gentle disagreement.

" "

court: 'I'm just a civil servant – what about you?' Or, if he knew the answer, 'I'm a civil servant, but what you do sounds much more interesting. Do tell me about it.'

There may be other reasons for being unwilling to talk about your job. Perhaps you are an estate agent, a traffic warden or something else that is often the butt of jokes or resentment; or you do something confidential in government or in the City; or you don't want people to assume that you are very rich or very poor. Whatever your reason, have an alternative line of conversation ready.

It's worth noting that turning the focus of conversation back on the other person will almost always pay dividends. If you encourage them to talk about themselves and their enthusiasms, they will come away

What makes me interesting?

• What do I do in my spare time that I really enjoy?

• Where have I been on holiday or on a day out lately?

• What have I read or seen recently that made me think or made me laugh?

• Have my children or pets done anything that made me laugh or nearly got me into trouble (though Her Ladyship advises against using this in gatherings where other people don't have children or pets)?

• Have I overheard anything odd or funny lately?

• What's in bloom in my garden or in the local park?

believing that you are a truly interesting person, for the simple reason that they have had a good time talking to you. About themselves.

Don't confine preparation of this kind to a description of your job or a way of diverting attention from it. Think up answers to other questions, or imagine what you would reply to someone whose conversational opening was 'Tell me about you.' The instinctive (and slightly defensive) response, 'What would you like to know?' doesn't do much to advance a conversation with someone who doesn't know you from Adam (or Eve). You are looking for answers to the (unasked) question 'What's interesting about me?', to which Her Ladyship beseeches you not even to consider replying, 'Nothing much.' Think about the things that excite you. They will, of course, vary enormously from person to person, but the box opposite has a few suggestions to get you started.

If anybody asks you about any of these things, you'll have something to say. Concentrate on what enthuses you and is likely to enthuse other people. Think around your subject, looking at it from different angles. Even the much-maligned trainspotting can be made to sound interesting to an outsider if you can talk about something other than engine numbers: perhaps you have had the opportunity to drive a train, or had a journey on a newly reopened steam railway, or been impressed by the revamping of an old station. People who have zero interest in trainspotting may still be able to empathise with these aspects of it.

Of course you don't have to talk exclusively about yourself. If you find yourself in a place of historic interest, for example, read up a little about it. Then, if you are in Bath and sitting next to someone who is waxing eloquent about its Regency architecture, you won't have to sit in shamefaced silence: you'll be able to throw in an informed observation or two before steering the conversation round to Jane Austen or the Roman baths if they are more comfortable territory. Bath is perhaps a bad example because it is so rich in possibilities, but the merest glance at the Internet will reveal interesting information about almost anywhere: Wolverhampton, for example, was the site of a battle between Anglo-Saxons and Danes in the days of Alfred the Great; Wakefield

saw a major battle in the Wars of the Roses, is now home to a Barbara
Hepworth museum and is renowned for its rhubarb; Ipswich was once
a famous pilgrimage destination and is the birthplace of Henry VIII's
Cardinal Wolsey. These are all things that you could ask a local about.
Her Ladyship does not mean to imply there is anything wrong with
Wolverhampton, Wakefield or Ipswich when giving these examples – she
merely means that a little investigation into places with less obvious
charms than Bath will pay dividends.

Cultivating a broad general knowledge is another way of finding
things to talk about. The story goes that a certain high-class 'escort
service' insisted that its employees read a serious newspaper every day,

> **66**
>
> **Having at least a vague idea of what
> is going on in the world will reduce
> your risk of feeling out of your depth
> the moment anyone starts discussing
> current affairs.**
>
> **99**

so that they had something to talk to their politician or tycoon clients
about. The clients were always flattered – as who wouldn't be? – that
their paid companions took such an interest in their work. While Her
Ladyship is not suggesting that you should memorise the share prices of
the FTSE 100 or the details of the latest government White Paper before
every social occasion, she does recommend extending your knowledge
beyond the realm of reality TV. Having at least a vague idea of what is
going on in the world will reduce your risk of feeling out of your depth
the moment anyone starts discussing current affairs.

Even if you are not employed by an escort agency, flattery or
deferring to another person's supposed superior knowledge can be a
useful thing in the early stages of a conversation, whatever your gender
or the gender of your conversational partner. Saying something like, 'I

heard something about that on the radio, but only the headline – what's going on?', is likely to encourage the other person to feel more confident, to relax and chat more easily.

You're not 'just' anything

Don't begin a sentence with 'I'm just a …' Not all of us can be brain surgeons: who would balance the books or build the houses if we were? Express pride in what you do. One friend of Her Ladyship's, in her thirties and a stay-at-home parent through choice, went to a school reunion. She was asked more than once by career-oriented peers, 'What are you doing these days?' and could have said, 'I'm just a housewife.' Being made of sterner stuff, she replied with a laugh, 'I expect I work harder than any of you. I look after three children.' Yes, she reported, one high-flying solicitor gave her a pitying look, but the others were frankly envious and happy to discuss her experiences of 'working' life.

" "

And what do you do?

I'm just a secretary.

Awkward silence.

And what do you do?

I work for the Sales Director of a stationery company.

Is that interesting?

Not really.

Awkward silence. But this shouldn't happen if you have come prepared.

Is that interesting?

Not really, but we have our moments. You've no idea how difficult people can be about the colour of their envelopes. There was a customer last week who ...

As long as this anecdote is entertaining, you are up and running. Alternatively, try:

Is that interesting?

Not really, but it helps pay the bills. We have two children at university and I'm sure you know how expensive that is.

I do indeed. My son's 17 and we have that to look forward to next year ...

Success! You have found something in common and avoided having to talk about your job.

66 99

Insider speak

Another way in which you can prepare yourself is if you know you are going to be an outsider – a non-scientist, say, in a group of scientists. Read at least the headlines of the science pages of the day's paper. Your understanding need only be superficial, as long as you know enough to ask the person you are talking to what he or she thinks. That person will think you are more interesting because you can take an interest in his or her field.

A tip for outsiders, though: find other outsiders. If you've been dragged along to a scientific party by your scientific partner, you can be reasonably confident that others have been too. Rather than trying to butt in on an animated science conversation, keep an eye open for someone else who looks out of their depth and talk to them. It would be the height of rudeness to interrupt a group of people who were talking about science and begin describing your experience at last weekend's gymkhana.

And a tip for insiders: it's easy, when talking about your work, to slip into jargon. Seek out the happy medium between baffling and patronising. A scientist who goes into detail about electron quasiparticles to non-scientists will soon find them shuffling their feet and staring into the bottom of their glass; one who asks, 'Do you know what DNA is?' has, in most adult circles, taken her dumbing down too far.

'I'm, like, so not interested in ...'

Conversation isn't an exercise in public speaking or a test of
your ability to put together a fluent sentence, but it's still worth
making an effort to avoid the worst clichés. A few years ago, 'like'
and 'whatever' were voted the two most irritating words in the
English language. If you have to say that you aren't interested in
something (which is not the most helpful conversational remark
at the best of times), do try to phrase it more elegantly. 'I don't
know much about' is hugely preferable to 'I'm not interested in',
and gives you the opportunity to introduce something in the same
general field that you are interested in: 'I don't know much about
Formula One', for example, 'but I am interested in horse-racing'
or 'I don't know much about archaeology, I'm afraid – I don't go
back much further than the Tudors.'

'Whatever', used in today's dismissive sense, is simply a ruder
version of 'I don't agree – think what you like' and shouldn't be
used unless you are intending to be offensive.

English is full of more-or-less meaningless fillers like these.
'As a matter of fact', 'actually', 'to tell you the truth', 'you know
what I mean' are other common examples. We all use them and
there is no serious harm in them; sometimes they are just a way
of allowing us to gather our thoughts before saying something
worthwhile. Her Ladyship is not proposing that you should
eliminate these expressions from your vocabulary entirely:
putting that sort of guard on your tongue would be a real barrier
to conversation. She merely suggests that keeping them to a
minimum ensures that the meaningless fillers don't overshadow
the meaningfulness of what you are trying to say.

Practise, practise, practise

If, despite the above recommendations, you remain nervous of talking to strangers and feel you have no small talk, make yourself practise. Start conversations in shops or bus queues, in the gym or in an art gallery.

In a museum or gallery, make a passing remark to someone who is taking an interest in the same object as you are. Admire the way the artist has captured the sunlight or the expression on his subject's face; express amazement that such exquisite pots or jewellery could have been produced thousands of years ago. It doesn't matter what you say, as long as it gives the other person a chance to respond. If they don't want to talk they'll nod briefly and walk away, and you will have lost nothing. If they do, you can share opinions and impressions until it's time to move on.

> **66**
> **As you hand over the jumper or necklace you are about to pay for, remark to the sales assistant that it's a lovely fabric or colour or style.**
> **99**

Ask the person next to you in the gym how they are getting on, how often they come here, whether they find the treadmill helps them lose weight. Ask it casually, expressing a friendly interest. You don't want to turn it into a grilling.

If you aren't a museum or gym person, try telling the man in the greengrocer's that the cherries you bought last week were delicious and ask what he recommends today. He'll be pleased and, not only will you buy good fruit, you'll feel pleased too. As you hand over the jumper or necklace you are about to pay for, remark to the sales assistant that it's a lovely fabric or colour or style. When buying a newspaper, say something about the headlines, the latest sporting event – even, if you must, the celebrity gossip. The people you are dealing with are bound to have something to say in response and you can pass a moment or two in an agreeable way.

Of course, this works only if both you and the other person have that moment or two to spare: don't try it when there is a queue building up behind you, and people are tutting with impatience. But when the circumstances are right, it's surprising how easy – and how pleasant – it is to exchange pleasantries.

If you have access to a dog, striking up conversations with other dog-owners is another tried-and-tested way to practise your skills. What age, what breed, does he run away when let off the lead? – these are all subjects on which dog-owners can wax lyrical. The same applies to anyone pushing a pram or pushchair, though Her Ladyship advises against asking a parent or grandparent what breed their baby is. Unadulterated admiration of the little one is the best way to start here.

A word of warning, though. It is perfectly reasonable to begin a conversation of this sort by addressing the dog or the baby, but do have the courtesy to include the adult companion.

This is one set of circumstances in which introductions aren't essential (see page 50 for more about this). A friend of Her Ladyship's once realised that she had been chatting to a fellow dog-owner in her local park several times a week for six months and knew perfectly well

> **"**
> **… when the circumstances are**
> **right, it's surprising how easy – and**
> **how pleasant – it is to exchange**
> **pleasantries.**
> **"**

that her dogs were springer/cocker crosses called Ruby and Pearl, but she had never discovered the woman's name. This didn't matter in the slightest until the day her father came out walking with her and she was unable to introduce her park acquaintance to him. She passed it off

Learn from the experts

If there is a television interviewer who you admire, watch them
and see how they do it. You'll find that they have done their
research (or employed a good researcher) and know enough about
their guest to ask intelligent questions. But the best of them are
also very strong on empathy: without talking about themselves or
interrupting their guest's flow of speech, they somehow manage to
convey that they recognise that situation and understand how the
other person must feel. Yes, it's a gift – good interviewers, like
good conversationalists generally, are surely born with a genuine
interest in what others have to say – but it's also a skill that can
be cultivated. Try it.

lightly by saying, 'Isn't it silly? I feel I know you so well.' The woman
responded without rancour or embarrassment – after all, she had never
asked Her Ladyship's friend's name either and their conversation hadn't
been at all inhibited as a result.

Although dogs and babies are widely recognised as excellent
springboards to conversation with strangers in public places, one
friend of Her Ladyship's also found that she had lots of friendly chats
when she had her leg in plaster after a skiing accident. Her Ladyship
acknowledges that deliberately breaking your leg in order to practise
talking to people would be rather drastic – she merely suggests that,
should it happen, you consider taking advantage of it.

Yes, you may argue, but firstly, I'm not frightened of these people, nor
am I trying to impress them; and secondly I'd be speaking to them for a
few minutes at most, not trying to sustain a lengthy conversation.

It doesn't matter, says Her Ladyship. It's not about making new best
friends or wowing strangers with your artistic knowledge. It's about

getting into the habit of finding other people interesting and affable. A surprising number of them are.

What's the worst that can happen?

This is a question worth asking yourself when you are truly nervous about a forthcoming event. And it's undeniable that awkward things can happen.

To take an extreme example, on his first visit to one of the hero's legendary parties, the narrator of F. Scott Fitzgerald's *The Great Gatsby* wandered around ill at ease among 'swirls and eddies' of people he didn't know. He asked a few people where the host was, but they 'stared at me in such an amazed way, and denied so vehemently any knowledge of his movements, that I slunk off in the direction of the cocktail table – the only place in the garden where a single man could linger without looking purposeless and alone.' Eventually someone he knew came to rescue him, but by this time he was 'on my way to roaring drunk from sheer embarrassment'. If you have read the book you will know that it was all downhill from there.

> **66**
> **Even if you are never likely to be exposed to Gatsbyesque excess, you can hit stumbling blocks – occasions when all the conversational skills in the world won't help you.**
> **99**

Even if you are never likely to be exposed to Gatsbyesque excess, you can hit stumbling blocks – occasions when all the conversational skills in the world won't help you. A friend of Her Ladyship's, married to a theatrical casting director, endured years of snubbing at first nights and other star-studded parties: the moment an actor realised she was 'only'

Mrs X and was not likely to be casting them in her next production, she was given very short shrift. This was despite the fact that she was distinguished in her own, less glitzy field: the people she was meeting seemed never to acknowledge the existence of a world outside the theatre. They also appeared not to give a thought to how easily she could have put in a good or bad word for them with her husband.

She was also often asked (by people who had not yet established that she was 'only' Mrs X), 'What would I have seen you in?' Out of respect for her husband, she usually refrained from replying, 'Sainsbury's? Or Harrods when there's a sale on?'

Her Ladyship's advice to anyone in that situation is, if at all possible, don't go. Unless moral support is absolutely essential, tell your partner

> **66**
>
> **If you find yourself repeatedly
> snubbed when attending your
> partner's functions, Her Ladyship's
> advice is, if at all possible,
> don't go.**   **99**

you are washing your hair that night, or make their business commitment an excuse to see a different set of friends. You'll be spared a lot of boredom, catch up with your own friends – and possibly have very clean hair. If you have to go, insist that your partner introduce you to someone compatible before they disappear to 'work the room'. If they are in a business where contacts are all-important, then obviously they must make the most of these opportunities, but that is no excuse for leaving you to be insulted by any passing wannabe.

This advice, of course, applies to both genders and to other occupations, but the situation is most likely to arise in the so-called 'glamorous' professions where chatting people up over a glass of warm white wine can be every bit as important as one's ability to do the job.

Not insulted, just ignored

Another friend of Her Ladyship's tells a different style of 'what's the worst that can happen?' story. He was invited to an early evening drinks party at the home of someone he knew slightly through work. It was an opportunity to do a bit of networking and he felt he should put in an appearance. He walked into a crowded room where he recognised not a single face. Some 60 people seemed to be engrossed in conversation, not remotely interested in him. He acquired a glass of wine to fortify himself and toured the room, looking in vain for his host. 'This is awful,' he thought. 'What am I going to do?'

What he did was retire to the loo, glass in hand, and spend ten minutes reading the evening paper. Then he emerged, hoping that someone he knew would have appeared while he was away from the fray. But no. He did another unsuccessful circuit, knocked back his wine and went home.

> **66**
> **If something utterly dreadful happens to you, shrug it off, put it down to experience and, in due course, turn it into an anecdote.**
> **99**

'It was utterly dreadful,' he told Her Ladyship. 'But it meant I had an evening at home, saw my wife, saw my daughter, did some paperwork. For half an hour it felt like the end of the world, but in the greater scheme of things it was really no big deal. And where the host was, why he didn't have the courtesy to be hosting his own party, I don't know to this day.'

Perhaps he was modelling himself on Jay Gatsby, but that is not, in Her Ladyship's view and outside the pages of a novel, any way for a host to behave.

The point to be noted here, though, is that the world didn't come to an end as a result of this episode. It rarely does. If something like this happens to you, shrug it off, put it down to experience and – in due course, when the embarrassment has faded – turn it into an anecdote that you and your friends can laugh over, or even put into a book.

Introductions and Getting Started

There was a pause. The conversation, to Bill's concern, showed signs of flagging. He saw that he must make an effort to brighten it, or it would expire in its tracks.
'Have you met any interesting cats lately?' he asked.

P. G. Wodehouse

"

I n the days of debutantes and 'coming out' balls, a young man might ask his hostess to introduce him to a young lady whose appearance had taken his fancy, but that was in the unlikely event that he didn't know her already. Bright young things all belonged to the same social circle and attended the same endless round of social events, so if you met someone at a party, the chances were that you or one of your siblings had been to school with them, or at the very least that you had met them at a party the previous week.

In these more open-minded and socially mobile times, we are more likely to come across people about whom we know nothing, which is why introductions are so important. Introducing yourself to strangers is probably number one on the list of factors that make unwilling partygoers tremble in their shoes, so an attentive host should strive to avoid leaving these timorous people to their own devices.

> 66
> **In these more open-minded and socially mobile times, we are more likely to come across people about whom we know nothing, which is why introductions are so important.**
> 99

At a private party, of course, it is likely to be one of the hosts who opens the door, greets you and brings you into the thick of things. You may also have established in advance who is going to be there and whom you might know or be eager to meet. On a more formal or business occasion, you may have to give your name to someone on the door, as a precaution against gatecrashers, but having done so you may simply walk in and have to sink or swim on your own. If this is the case, seek a host out as soon as possible and say hello. As well as being good manners, in a business context this is a good tactic: the host will register that you have bothered to turn up and that will be a point in your or your firm's favour. (Her Ladyship is constantly amazed by the number of people who accept invitations to business functions – and even occasionally to private ones – and then stay away without notifying

anyone. As well as being abominably rude, it throws the catering
arrangements into chaos.)

If nothing better occurs to you, perhaps because you don't know the
host very well, make a friendly remark complimenting the room, the
décor or the fact that the party seems to be going with a swing. Don't
attempt to embark on a serious conversation or a business pitch: you
can't expect a busy host to stay chatting to you long enough for this to
be other than frustrating. But he or she should at least take the time to
make sure you know enough people to feel comfortable; if you don't, your
host should make a point of introducing you to someone congenial. If it
looks as if this is not going to happen, overcome your embarrassment,
confess that you don't know many of your fellow guests and ask who you
should be talking to. This should remind the most preoccupied host
of his or her obligations.

Performing introductions

At a business-related party Her Ladyship attended recently, she was
greeted in the entrance hall by a young woman – let's call her Lisa –
who worked for the host company. Lisa showed Her Ladyship where to
leave her coat, waited to escort her into the party, caught the attention
of a passing waiter in order to give her a drink and enquired if she
knew people. Her Ladyship asked to be introduced to someone she had
'met' only by email – and not until this was done and Lisa was sure Her
Ladyship was happy did she return to her post, to perform the same
service for the next arrival. The whole process took less than three
minutes, but it was a masterclass in how to meet and greet. Had Her
Ladyship not known anyone, she is sure that Lisa would have introduced
her to someone, explained to both parties who the other was and – this
is the key here – given them a hint as to why they might be interested in
talking to each other.

Whatever function you are hosting, whether private or business, formal or casual, introductions are a vital part of your duties. Don't just mention names: 'Robin, this is Andy – Andy, Robin' doesn't help Andy or Robin much at all. 'Robin, this is my old college chum Andy. Andy, Robin's just started work at the office' gives them something much more concrete to go on. Robin can ask Andy which college it was and what he studied; Andy can ask what Robin does within the organisation and where he was before. It's even better if you can tell the people you are introducing that they have something in common – a shared interest in travel or cooking or cinema, for instance. They can then ask each other where they have been lately, what their favourite cuisine is or what they think of Tarantino's latest. Once this exchange is under way, you can safely leave them to it. They don't need to stick to that particular subject for any length of time – you have simply given them a starting-off point in the hope that real and spontaneous conversation will spring from it.

> 66
> Whatever function you are hosting, whether private or business, formal or casual, introductions are a vital part of your duties.
> 99

Introducing yourself

The same guidelines apply if you are introducing yourself to someone. Tell them something about yourself: in a business context this could be your company name or job title; at a private party, the fact that you are the host's sister/cousin/colleague/bridge partner. It's not that you specifically want to talk about work or bridge or, God forbid, your relations: you're giving the other person a clue as to what to talk to you about.

If you're feeling shy about approaching people, look out for someone who is not deep in conversation. You can tell by the way people are

If you seek a subject, look around you

If you're lucky enough to be at a party in a handsome location,
you can temporarily disguise the fact that you are on your own
by wandering round admiring the chandeliers, the fireplace or
the paintings on the wall, and possibly fall into conversation
with someone else doing the same thing. But the venue doesn't
have to be grand. Her Ladyship once attended a party in an
unpretentious church hall that doubled as a kindergarten; a panel
on one wall was covered with photos of the children and lists of
their food allergies. She got talking to a man she didn't know who
was fascinated by these lists. One of the pupils was apparently
allergic to mango and another to quinoa. 'When I was four,' the
man said, after expressing sympathy for the children's plight, 'I'd
never heard of either of those, and I still can't pronounce one of
them.' It led to an interesting discussion on exotic foodstuffs and
the sophistication of today's four-year-olds. Conversational topics
can be found in surprising places if you think to look for them.

In a private home, the hosts' bookshelves or CD collections
will often provide a rich source of material: only a fellow book-
or music-lover is likely to be looking at them, so you can be
reasonably sure of having something in common. If someone asks
you if you have read a book (or seen a film or anything else of
that sort) that you haven't, a good response is always, 'No. Should
I?', encouraging the other person to tell you their views.

standing – facing each other and maintaining eye contact – if they are in an earnest discussion that shouldn't be interrupted. Look instead for a group that seems less intense, where there may be a gap in the circle that you can be welcomed into. Smile, say, 'Do you mind if I join you?', introduce yourself and you should find you are accepted. Don't force your way headlong into the conversation at this point – let the people who are already talking carry on, but feel free to interject the odd comment if it feels appropriate and non-invasive.

> **If you're feeling shy about approaching people, look out for someone who is not deep in conversation.**

Alternatively, go up to someone who seems to be alone. Be open about the fact that you are on your own too. If you just tell this person your name, it could throw them into a panic. Are they supposed to know who you are? Are you someone with whom they should curry favour? Are you – dreadful thought – the CEO of the company hosting the party, nobly doing the rounds of the guests? Or are you just another lonely soul looking for someone to talk to? If you say, 'You look as if you're on your own. I am too. Terrifying, isn't it? But isn't this a lovely room?' they may be astonishingly grateful.

Fancy dress

Her Ladyship confesses to a passionate loathing of fancy-dress parties. However, she admits that they have one redeeming feature: they allow you to go up to a stranger and ask who they are meant to be without it sounding rude. But do try to avoid the obvious: if you ask someone dressed as a pirate where his parrot is, or someone dressed as Robin Hood if he has robbed any interesting rich people lately, you may think you are being witty. But so did the six people who have already asked that question in the course of the evening.

Get the name right

When you're introduced to someone, particularly in a noisy environment, it's perfectly reasonable to ask them to repeat their name, to make sure you have it right: say something like 'Sorry, I didn't catch that – you are …?' You may then like to use the name, to reinforce it in your own mind: 'Nice to meet you, Fiona.' But do this once only: overdoing it – 'Nice to meet you, Fiona. And tell me, Fiona, what do you do? Isn't this a lovely party, Fiona?' – will suggest that you think Fiona is the most ridiculous name you have ever heard and won't endear you to your new acquaintance.

If you're unsure how to address someone – particularly someone older – err on the side of caution and formality. Call a friend's parents Mr and Mrs Francis until and unless they invite you to call them Richard and Julia. If the person concerned happens to have a title, try to use the correct form. Address a duke or duchess as 'Duke' and 'Duchess', but don't call an earl 'Earl'. Peers below the rank of duke (that is, in descending order, marquesses, earls, viscounts and barons) and their wives, as well as life peers of both sexes, should be addressed as 'Lord' or 'Lady' followed by their surname; a knight is Sir Michael and a dame is Dame Angela. More complicated are the children of peers: the eldest son usually has a title of his own, while daughters and younger sons are addressed as Lady Harriet or Lord Christopher. If in doubt, ask, 'What should I call you?' and then do as they request.

> **"** If you're unsure how to address someone – particularly someone older – err on the side of caution and formality. **"**

Similarly, if someone is introduced by the full version of a name that has a common abbreviation and the occasion itself is not a very formal one, feel free to say something like 'Nice to meet you, James. Or are you Jamie? Or Jim?' But don't address this man as Jamie or Jim

until he has confirmed that that is what he prefers: if he is Jamie only
to his family, he will think you are being overfamiliar. Remarking on
an unusual name, as long as it is done in a pleasant and enquiring way,
can be a starting point for conversation: if you discover that Demelza or
Claudette or Daniela has connections with Cornwall or Quebec or Peru,
you can ask interested questions or share your own experiences – and
if you can talk to someone called Demelza without mentioning *Poldark*
she will be your slave for life. Be aware that, as with the fancy-dress
witticisms mentioned above, you will not be the first person in Demelza's
experience to make this connection.

As a final point on this subject, do try to make the distinction
between similar-sounding names. Her Ladyship speaks from bitter
experience when she assures you that calling a Caroline Carolyn or a
Maria Marie will annoy the women concerned considerably more than
forgetting their name altogether.

I think we've met

Going up to someone and saying something along the lines of 'I'm sure
we've met but I'm sorry, I don't remember your name. I'm ...' can be
a useful gambit, whether or not you think you have encountered them
before. They will naturally introduce themselves and tell you a bit about
themselves, and you will have surmounted the first hurdle.

Her Ladyship once had an amusing experience of this well-meaning
approach. A friend of hers was indisposed and unable to accompany her
solicitor husband to a lunch party, so Her Ladyship was invited instead.
Lawyers, accountants, architects and others – almost exclusively men –
who had been involved in the development of a new conference centre
were celebrating, with their partners, the near-completion of what had
been a long and tricky project. Her Ladyship had never met any of them,
but on two separate occasions in the course of the afternoon women came
up to her and said how nice it was to see her again. Both turned out to be

the wives of professionals involved in the project: they had been to the 'completion of phase one' and 'completion of phase two' parties, but – barring their own husbands, who were talking shop – they didn't know anyone in the room very well. 'Nice to see you again' was their tentative approach to someone whom they assumed they had met at the previous gatherings.

Her Ladyship felt that she rose to the occasion. She introduced herself, asked to be reminded of her new acquaintances' names and observed, of the conference centre, 'It's looking wonderful, isn't it? They must all be so proud – and so pleased that it's nearly over.' The supportive wives responded enthusiastically and Her Ladyship was able to embark on a friendly, if undemanding, conversation about what the men were likely to be doing next and whether their wives would be glad to see more of them. A strict adherence to the facts would have meant her embarrassing her companions by assuring them that they had never met before. It was one of those moments when economy with the truth paid social dividends (see White Lies, page 98).

This incident took place many years ago, and Her Ladyship does sometimes speculate as to whether it would have occurred today, when a substantial number of the professionals are likely to have been female and some of the supportive partners male. She likes to think that she might have discussed the building's design with the female architect, leaving the men to say how nice it was to see each other again and talk about golf.

When your memory lets you down

Assuming you've met someone you haven't is unlikely to give offence; forgetting that you have met someone before is more awkward, particularly if they seem to remember you well. A quick apology along the lines of 'How stupid of me – I'm so bad at names' should smooth things over.

If you are the person who has been forgotten, Her Ladyship beseeches you to be gracious. A friend of hers was once submitted to an extreme example of *un*graciousness in just such a situation. The man she offended was someone about whom she had heard a lot, not all of it complimentary, but she said enthusiastically that she was delighted to meet him at last. He replied, 'I met you once.' And then said absolutely nothing else.

Had he added, 'It was at my cousin's wedding' or 'It was at a big party, I don't blame you for forgetting' or even 'I'm not sure when, but I know your face', the awkwardness would have passed quickly. As it was, it hung in the air for several moments, until Her Ladyship's friend decided that she needed a breath of air, excused herself and went out into the garden, never to return. That was a conversation – and a relationship – that did not prosper.

Names don't always matter

As illustrated by the dogs in the park story on page 34, it isn't essential to know someone's name in order to strike up a friendly conversation with them. Yes, it makes sense to be able to address someone by name if you are going to spend any length of time with them (at a dinner table, for example), but there are plenty of circumstances in which this is less important. Imagine being part of a group emerging from a concert and gathering in the bar or in the queue for a taxi. It's very easy to say to someone standing next to you, 'Wasn't that fabulous?' and for that person

66 99

Hello, I'm Helen, I don't think we've met.

I did meet you once.

Awkward silence.

Hello, I'm Helen, I don't think we've met.

I did meet you once. I'm Mark, Rob's cousin. It was at Rob's birthday party but you were a bit distracted: I think you had a presentation the next day.

Of course, I remember. How rude of me. I had to go to London and I was terrified that I was going to oversleep and miss the train.

And did you?

No, it was fine. Actually I had a really good day...

Notice how Mark not only reminds Helen of who he is and where they have met, but gives her an excuse for having forgotten. As long as Helen talks about herself only briefly before saying to Mark, 'And what about you? What have you been doing since we met?', a conversation is launched.

66 99

to respond, 'I particularly liked the contralto – what a wonderfully rich voice.' If you have any views on the contralto – you liked her, you heard her in *The Messiah* last year, you preferred the soprano – you can chatter away without bothering about your companion's name. Then if anyone comes to join you, you can simply say, 'I'm sorry – I didn't catch your name' and leave them to introduce themselves.

Similarly, if you find yourself next to a friendly looking stranger at the races, you can venture a remark on the course, the weather or your thoughts for the 3.30. At a garden party it's easy to comment on the floral display and how beautiful it is at this time of year. Then see what the other person has to say. Again, there is no need for introductions here. After all, a person's name (provided you don't get it wrong) is only a small part of their persona: knowing it is not a prerequisite to exchanging views on contraltos, racing or herbaceous borders. As one expert has remarked – with reference to talking to someone standing at the bar in a pub, another occasion when introducing yourself by name is unnecessary – 'the object is to "drift" casually into conversation, as if by accident'.

This is, according to the same expert, something that Americans and others of a more outgoing nature find difficult to understand. The American habit of going up to a stranger, offering a broad smile and outstretched hand and saying, 'Hi, I'm Jed Gould from Fargo, North Dakota; I'm in agricultural machinery' may be acceptable at a business conference but sits uncomfortably in the British social scene – and would be decidedly off-putting if you were standing at the bar in a pub.

Breaking the ice

So you've said hello and told a stranger who you are. That, in chess
terms, is Pawn to King 4. The other player will probably counter with
exactly the same move. Her Ladyship – no chess player – suggests that
any six-year-old can do that. It's what you do next that matters.

Throughout the centuries, many people, particularly those who fancy
themselves as intellectuals, have claimed to be bad at 'small talk'. When
making this statement, they always manage to imply that small talk is
beneath them, that their brains are too lofty to deal with passing the
time of day. It may well be that the average particle physicist has little
to say that would interest the average sociologist or socialite, but the
best conversationalists, it has been
said, are those who are genuinely
interested in other people and
experience real delight in finding
out about their lives, rather than
imparting their own knowledge of
particle physics.

> **The best conversationalists, it has been said, are those who are genuinely interested in other people and experience real delight in finding out about their lives.**

The very name small talk, of
course, is disparaging. But the point
of it is not to keep conversation on
a banal, chit-chatty level. That's
one of the ways in which things have changed since *Pygmalion*, as
mentioned in the introduction, was written a century ago. Then, Professor
Higgins' intention was to keep his unproven protégée away from the
dangerous waters of interesting conversation – nowadays, we use small
talk as a way to test out those waters and find some solid ground. One
twentieth-century philosopher divided communication into five levels,
of which 'cliché conversation' – small talk on the 'How are you? How's
the family?' level – was the lowest. From here, he said, you progressed
through reporting facts, expressing opinions and admitting to emotions
until you reached 'peak communication', by which point you were

perfectly in tune with the other person. His thesis was that people keep their exchanges on the clichéd level out of fear of opening up to others. That may well be so, but Her Ladyship views this sort of exchange as a means to an end. She is not suggesting that you will achieve peak communication in every conversation that begins 'Do you come here often?'; what she is saying is that if you don't start with questions like that, you will never get anywhere.

Her advice, therefore, is not to despise small talk and not to be afraid of banal questions. 'How do you know your host?' or 'Where do you fit into the organisation?' acts as a conversational baton; with any luck, the other person will pick it up and run with it. (Those sporting metaphors keep slipping in, she finds.) Questions like this have the advantage of being 'open' (or 'open-ended') – that is, they require the other person to answer something more than 'yes' or 'no'. A question like 'Have you had far to come?' is, strictly speaking, 'closed', but a friendly person will recognise it as the gambit it is meant to be and treat it openly. If that person says, 'No, I live just round the corner', it enables you to remark that it's a pleasant neighbourhood and ask if they've lived there long. Or, if they have had to come a long way, they can explain the circumstances or ask you if you know their home town.

A less friendly person, of course, can give a monosyllabic answer, so you need to be prepared to follow up your initial question with something more exploratory.

As an alternative opener, don't be afraid of compliments, particularly woman to woman: very few women are going to be offended if you admire their brooch or their shoes. But content yourself with admiring – leave it to them to decide whether or not to tell you where they bought it (they may not care to admit that it was ludicrously expensive or ludicrously cheap). The idea, as so often, is to open a conversation, not to submit a stranger to the third degree. And beware of gushing: if you tell someone you love her dress, she is likely to be pleased; if she then overhears you saying precisely the same thing to the person standing next to her, she may be less impressed.

“ ”

Have you come far?

No.

Awkward silence.

Have you come far?

No.

So you're local. It's a beautiful town, isn't it? Have you lived here long?

All my life.

You must love it very much.

Not really – I just can't afford to move anywhere more exciting.

Oh dear. It might be time to make your excuses. But you could have one more try.

I noticed an odd sort of monument by the roundabout as I drove up – do you know the one I mean?

Oh yes, that's to do with the Civil War. One of the early Royalist victories was just down the road – we're very proud of Charles I round here.

Really? I didn't know anyone was proud of Charles I. Tell me more.

Aha! Assuming you are prepared to feel – or feign – interest in Charles I for a few minutes, you may have struck gold.

“ ”

If someone accosts you with this sort of remark, respond encouragingly. An answer such as 'Oh this old thing', accompanied by a shrug of the shoulders, will make the other person feel uncomfortable, which is, by definition, bad manners. Try, 'Oh, thank you. It was a present from…' or (assuming that you didn't buy it in a prohibitively expensive designer outlet or on holiday in the Maldives) 'I bought it in …' – open-ended replies that give the other person an opportunity to carry on talking.

What are we going to talk about?

Nothing is too trivial to be used at this early stage, when you might feel you are floundering for something to say. Even an apparently trite observation on the dreadful weather may provoke someone else to remark that this time next week they will be in Corfu – and a real conversation can flow from there.

To enlarge on what Her Ladyship means by 'real' conversation, she cannot do better than give an example from her own recent experience, when she spent a weekend with friends in the country. These friends invited some neighbours, whom Her Ladyship had never met, to go walking with them on the Saturday and join them for an evening meal. In the course of ten hours, the conversation ranged easily over such topics as keeping bees, the merits of English sparkling wine, what fun (but how tiring) it was having the grandchildren to stay, and whether or not it would be exciting to go up in a rocket and see the Earth from space. None of these would necessarily have been on a prescribed list of 'suitable topics'. They arose because everyone concerned was enthusiastic about what they were doing with life and was happy to talk about it, but also because they were prepared to be interested in what the others of the group had to say. There is no better recipe for stimulating conversation than that. Though it may be that the English sparkling wine helped a little.

" "

Miserable day, isn't it?

Yes.

Awkward silence.

Miserable day, isn't it?

Yes.

I just hope it clears up before Wimbledon starts.

I'm really not that interested in tennis.

Oh? Are you interested in any sports?

No.

What do you do in your spare time, then?

Your taciturn acquaintance can't answer yes or no to this question – he has to open up a little, or be downright rude.

I collect matchboxes.

Really? I don't know anything about matchboxes. What's collectible about them?

Who knows? You may learn something.

" "

If someone you are trying to talk to won't meet you halfway, you are going to run out of steam sooner or later, however determined a talker you are. As mentioned in the Introduction, conversation founders when other people don't show any interest in you, when they don't flip the ball back into your court.

Perhaps the single most important contribution anyone can make to a conversation is to ask some variation on the theme of 'And what about you?' This can take the form of 'What do you do?', 'Where are you from?', 'What do you think?', but it flatters the other person by suggesting that they might have something to say that you are happy to listen to. Not only that, it more or less forces them to say *something*.

And remember that you are looking for common ground with this person – it doesn't have to be relentlessly cheerful. What has been called 'shared moaning', particularly about the weather, can establish a bond every bit as easily as a mutual enthusiasm. Nor do you have to talk about how exciting your life is or how exotic your travels: a shared experience needn't be hiking the Inca Trail – it can equally well be a hatred of the queues in your local supermarket.

> **If you are prepared to talk enthusiastically *and* to be interested in what others have to say there is no better recipe for stimulating conversation than that.**

" "

Miserable day, isn't it?

Yes.

It really gets you down, doesn't it? I got soaked walking the dogs yesterday.

Yes, and then it's such a pain getting them clean. I have a Yorkshire Terrier and she's impossible. She won't stand still to be brushed and she's such a mess when she gets muddy.

And I bet she leaps all over the furniture the moment she has the chance.

Absolutely. I should never have bought that cream sofa – even when she's clean she leaves hair all over it.

Neither of you has said anything remotely cheerful, but you are both having a perfectly good time, talking about something you have in common.

" "

Plan your getaway

If you are truly nervous about a social occasion, give yourself an escape route. Warn your host in advance that you may not be able to stay long – because your father is ill or you have to do a presentation tomorrow morning – and then give yourself a time limit: if you haven't found anyone you are happy to talk to within half an hour, take advantage of your excuse and leave. If you do find you are enjoying yourself and your host remarks on it at midnight, you can always say, 'Oh, he's much better, thank you' or 'I finished work early and got all my preparation done more quickly than I expected.' Obviously you shouldn't do this with a close friend or relation who knows that your father is playing golf in the Algarve or a colleague who knows that the presentation isn't until next week. But at a party where you don't know anyone well it can boost your confidence to know that you can run away if you need to – and therefore make it less likely that you will feel the need to run away.

What if you are really stuck?

One occasion when there is very little you can do is when you are sitting in your allocated place at a formal dinner, the people on either side of you are talking to their other neighbours and the table is too large to talk across. There was a time – in the days of rigid etiquette – when a gentleman always 'took' a lady down to dinner; she sat on his right and it was his duty to attend to her comfort, holding her chair for her and not sitting down himself until she was settled. This automatically gave each person at the table someone to talk to, but etiquette demanded that after a certain time they turned away from their allocated partner and conversed with their other neighbour (it was considered bad manners to talk to anyone across the table). Well-brought-up people seemed to manage to do this instinctively, extricating themselves from one conversation without giving offence and embarking smoothly on another.

Sadly, this sort of training is no longer given to potential dinner guests, and although most people sitting down at a table will have the courtesy to acknowledge both their neighbours and to include them in conversation, the sort of neglect just described does happen.

One of your options is simply to butt in, contributing your mite to whatever they are talking about. Obviously not everyone is comfortable with this and, if it doesn't work, you are worse off than before. More subtle, perhaps, is to ask one of your neighbours if they'd care for some bread or some salt or whatever happens to be to hand. If they know the rules they'll reciprocate with a polite acceptance or refusal, then offer you something that is within their reach but out of yours. An exchange as simple as this may lead to conversation. Introduce yourself and ask what their connection with the event is. The very fact that you are in the same place at the same time for the same reason should give you something to talk about. And, as in any other conversational setting, once you have set the ball rolling there is no need to talk exclusively about the event in question: the moment you find something that interests you both, you can be off in any direction you choose.

If this tactic doesn't work, you are, unfortunately, stuck with your own company until one of these insensitive people deigns to notice you or, at the absolute worst, until the formalities of the dinner are over. Stand up and move around at the earliest opportunity; seek out your partner, your host or someone else who is on their own – and hope that they will have better manners than your neighbours.

> **"**
> **An exchange as simple as asking your neighbour whether they would care for some bread may lead to conversation.**
> **"**

Perhaps even worse is to find yourself at a table where everyone but you seems to have gone to the same public school or to share views you find unacceptable on fox hunting or immigration. You are, unfortunately, more or less condemned to silence – there is no justification for making a scene and you are unlikely to win over this vocal majority with the tactics described on page 100. Her Ladyship's advice is to resist the temptation to commandeer all the wine on the table; excuse yourself as soon as possible; and remember, next year, to send a donation and plead a prior engagement.

Am I Boring You?

Perhaps the world's second-worst crime is boredom; the first is being a bore.

Cecil Beaton

H er Ladyship spoke earlier of the advantages of making and maintaining the right level of eye contact. She reintroduces the subject here because eye contact serves another useful purpose. It makes it easy to tell if someone else's eyes are glazing over.

Be honest with yourself: this is not likely to happen if the other person is doing most of the talking, or is enjoying batting the conversational ball back and forth with you. It happens because you are boring them.

Try to interrupt yourself before this happens. The old joke about the author who stops monopolising the conversation in order to ask, 'Well, enough about me – what did you think of my book?' is funny because it can seem uncomfortably close to home. If you are the guest of honour at a formal event it is safe to assume that people are interested in what you have to say; otherwise, remember to give others a chance every now and again.

You aren't the only expert

It is all too easy, when you are knowledgeable or enthusiastic about a subject, to assume that your knowledge and enthusiasm are unique, or at least superior to anyone else's. The following is a personal list, but Her Ladyship is always particularly irritated by people who seem to believe that they are the only person who:

- has ever travelled outside the USA or Western Europe
- knows one wine grape from another
- has been to an opera festival/read *War and Peace*/seen a rock icon in concert.

You may have your own pet hates. But to use only the examples on this list, if you boast about your travels you run the risk both of offending someone who went to Vietnam last summer (and may think your trip

Beware 'mansplaining'

This recently identified phenomenon is defined as the (alleged) compulsion a man feels to explain the simplest thing to a woman, on the basis that – as a woman – she is too stupid or too innocent to understand it without his help. Her Ladyship does not mean to become sidetracked into the realm of gender politics: she merely suggests that her male readers be careful not to be condescending and that her female ones be prepared, very occasionally, gently and only when truly provoked, to interject, 'Actually, I know that.'

to Oman isn't any great shakes) and of causing resentment in someone who took the kids camping in Dorset and got rained out (who may wish they had your sort of money, or may despise you for not recognising the simple pleasures to be found closer to home). You may be imparting what you think are pearls of wisdom about wine and the arts to an audience who knows just as much as you do, or you may be laying down the law to a group of tone-deaf beer drinkers who have sworn off Russian novels for political reasons. In either case you run the risk of coming across as a pretentious bore.

So am I boring you?

If you have to ask, the answer is probably yes. It's not difficult to assess if you have lost your audience, even if their eyes haven't actually glazed over. If they are looking over your shoulder for someone else to talk to or a waiter to get them another drink; scribbling and doodling rather than taking notes in a meeting; fidgeting and surreptitiously looking at their watch, it is very likely that you are saying the wrong thing in the wrong way, or simply going on too long. It's time to ask whatever variant of 'And what about you?' is best suited to the occasion.

> **In Her Ladyship's opinion, 'Am I boring you?' is perhaps the worst question anyone can ask in the course of conversation.**

In Her Ladyship's opinion, 'Am I boring you?' is perhaps the worst question anyone can ask in the course of conversation, with the question-cum-statement 'I'm quite boring, aren't I?' a close second. There is no answer to either: obviously no polite person will reply, 'Well, yes, you are, actually', however tempted they may be. But 'No, no, of course not' cannot help but sound insincere. Yet it's extraordinary how many poor conversationalists fall back on this self-pitying utterance.

Don't do it. If you have prepared yourself as suggested on pages 24–27, you shouldn't need to – you should have interesting things to say. If you feel you are talking too much or going on too long on the same theme, acknowledge it and change the subject before the other person begins to show a desire to scream. One conversation expert suggests that you liken your grip on a conversation to the boiling of an egg. If you have been holding forth for more than three minutes, it's time you stopped. Her Ladyship is inclined to think that even this is overdoing it. Think of the two minutes' silence held on Armistice Day or Memorial Day – that can seem like a surprisingly long time. Obviously she is not suggesting

Let's talk about me

An acquaintance of Her Ladyship's – an advertising copywriter in her day job – was an aspiring novelist by night. When a literary agent expressed interest in her attempt at romantic fiction, she decided that her own name was too prosaic: she wanted something that would sit comfortably on bookshelves alongside all the Zoes, Annabels and Lucys who dominated the genre at the time. 'I'm thinking of changing my name,' she announced at dinner parties, going on to explain the circumstances and ask for suggestions.

Her friends were only too eager to help and were happy to discuss whether she should become an Estella or a Belle or a Scarlett. Even so, after the budding author had initiated this conversation for the third time in as many weeks, her husband took her to task on the way home, observing that if she had said, 'Let's talk about me now' she could hardly have been more blatant. She was among friends and the subject under discussion was fun, but it would have been more tactful to throw the conversation open and ask what pen-names other people might choose to adopt should the situation arise.

you keep a stopwatch in your hand: merely that you should be sensitive to other people's lack of fascination with the sound of your voice.

Of course, you may be going on and on through nerves rather than arrogance, but the same advice applies. If you feel you can hear your voice 'echoing along a corridor', as it was once memorably described – if you are prattling on about who knows what because you are frightened of the awkward silence that will otherwise prevail – then do just stop. That potential silence is appreciably less awkward than the sound of your audience's jaws creaking in synchronised yawns.

Be careful to bring your monologue to a close with a light touch. If you can say, 'Well, I mustn't go boring on' without making it sound self-pitying, by all means do. If not, confine yourself to something neutral such as 'Well, enough about that.' Then give the other person a chance to talk. Ask what they have been doing today, what kind of music they like or if they are going away this summer. As is so often the case, it doesn't matter *what* you ask, as long as you ask as if you were interested in the answer and then listen to it attentively.

Give it a rest

Even if you're being fascinating (and remember that you are perhaps not the best judge of whether or not that is true), there's a limit to how much people want to listen to you. Her Ladyship once had to woo a peer of the realm who was also a noted polymath and television personality into 'fronting' a project in which she was involved. She took him to lunch in a smart London restaurant, in the company of the photographer whose work was to be showcased. The peer was extremely pleasant. He agreed to do everything that was asked of him and he held forth at some length on the theme of the photographs, about which he seemed to have an in-depth knowledge. He had an easy, fluent turn of phrase and a fund of good stories. Not the most hardened socialist could have accused him of being boring, or pompous, or arrogant. But it was clear that he was used to being the most intelligent and interesting person around and expected to do most of the talking.

When he left, the photographer heaved a deep sigh and asked Her Ladyship (it was in the days when you were allowed to smoke in restaurants), 'Do you mind if I have a cigarette? I actually gave up two years ago, but I'd really like one now.' Her Ladyship, a lifelong non-smoker, knew exactly how he felt and had another cup of coffee. The peer, for all his charm, had worn them both out.

Name-dropping

This unattractive habit should be avoided unless you can be amusing about it. If you are lucky enough to move in exalted circles, be aware that not everyone else does and that they may feel resentful if you seem to be boasting. If the people you are talking to *do* move in exalted circles, they won't be impressed by your dropping the names of people they know too. A friend of Her Ladyship's did a lot of charity work that frequently brought her into contact with royalty. Having been invited to a Buckingham Palace garden party on what turned out to be a very hot day, she was subsequently entertaining about the difficulty of preventing

> **Name-dropping is an unattractive habit that should be avoided unless you can be amusing about it.**

almost liquid ice cream from running down the front of her dress and the way her carefully applied make-up turned into a gooey mess. She didn't say, 'Of course, it was lovely to see Kate again' or anything else to suggest that meeting members of the Royal Family was a commonplace occurrence – even though to her it was. Self-deprecating humour will carry you a long way in circumstances like this.

Deflating a name-dropper isn't difficult, but again should be done with humour. If someone begins a story with, 'I went to Buckingham

Palace the other day', interject 'As one does' or 'The way you do.' This will indicate to the speaker that you are happy to hear the tale, but recognise that they are perhaps showing off just a little. Harsher, and only to be used with a chronic bragger, is 'Kate who?'

Over-apologising

Apologising for a genuine fault or imperfection is one thing; carrying on doing it can be boring for everyone else, as they feel obliged to keep on (and on) assuring you that whatever it is is all right really. In Her Ladyship's experience, this failing is particularly common with the nervous hostess who insists on drawing attention to the supposed shortcomings of the food she is serving. At one end of the scale, announcing that the lemon tart is 'only M&S' is rather demeaning to the person who has just remarked on how delicious it is. At the other, confessing that the partridge stuffed inside the swan isn't organic because Fortnum and Mason's had sold out is an indirect boast, and not a very indirect one at that.

Dealing with bores

Stopping yourself from being boring should, in theory, be easy enough. But what do you do when you're confronted with a bore?

While considering what to write in this section, Her Ladyship came across the following passage in a novel set in the nineteenth century. At her coming-of-age party, a young lady wishes to be alone with the hero, but another guest is intent on discussing a contentious matter with him:

> 'Mr S,' Kitty interrupted, in her most acidly polite voice, 'fascinating though this is, the evening runs on and I must not

A man walked into a pub …

Jokes may act as an ice-breaker in a best man's speech (though Her Ladyship begs leave to suggest that they are not a fail-safe even then). They can be fun among a group of friends in a pub. But in almost all other circumstances they aren't conversation. They are monologues. They give the teller the chance to shine without leaving anyone else an opportunity to contribute – unless they are simply waiting for the punchline in order to nip in with a joke of their own. This turns a monologue into a game of one-upmanship, which isn't conversation either.

If you do have a joke that you are longing to tell, tell it at the right moment and in the right company. Don't interrupt a serious conversation in order to be frivolous, and be as sure as you reasonably can that your audience – all your audience – will appreciate it. A badly told joke, a distasteful joke or a joke that not everyone understands is a real destroyer of conversation. Four out of five people may be convulsed, but if the fifth says, 'I'm sorry, I don't get it', the pleasure is lost. The person who doesn't 'get it' risks becoming the butt of the others' humour, and few things are less funny than a joke that has to be explained.

allow Mr W to occupy your time exclusively. Would you
pardon us?'

The unfortunate Mr S has no option but to 'swoop into an exaggerated bow' and allow the couple to move on.

This sort of tactic belongs to the days when, as another chronicler of a similar period wrote, nothing was ever a lady's fault. Also, as is obvious even from this brief passage, Kitty had no compunction about hurting Mr S's feelings. Nowadays, even a young lady celebrating her twenty-first birthday, and expecting her will to be law for the evening, should perhaps think twice before indulging in such high-handed behaviour.

On the other hand, there is a useful pointer to be gleaned from the incident: it is far more polite to suggest that you are monopolising the other person than to point out that he or she is monopolising you against your will. A charming smile accompanied by, 'I've taken up far too much of your time and I must let you get on', should allow you to make a dignified exit. Alternatively, if you are within touching (or, if you are truly at the end of your tether, calling) distance of someone you know,

> **"**
> **It is far more polite to suggest that you are monopolising the other person than to point out that he or she is monopolising you against your will.**
> **"**

try attracting their attention and introducing them into the conversation. 'This gentleman [use the bore's name if you know it] has been telling me all about the upgrades he's had to do on his computer: I'm sure you'll be fascinated. I've just got to powder my nose.'

Needless to say, you shouldn't return to that part of the room for some little time, because not only do you not want to be lured back into the conversation, you may find that you have lost a friend.

It's worth bearing in mind, though, that people who dominate the conversation or seem to have only one topic on which to expound are probably nervous or insecure in unfamiliar social situations. The friendly thing to do is to boost their confidence by taking something they have said and using it as a springboard to express your own take on it. If the subject is, indeed, computer upgrades, try saying something like 'Oh I know, it's dreadful, isn't it? I had to upgrade my system recently: I was terrified I'd overwrite everything I was working on ...' You are now launched into an anecdote of your own, but showing yourself in a modest light that shouldn't intimidate the other person. Or, if you know nothing about computers, try, 'There was a lot to be said for the old days, wasn't there? It's such a shame that we don't write letters any more − when did you last have anything interesting in the post?' The other person has to answer with something that isn't about computer upgrades, and you may succeed in drawing them out on a subject that is of more interest to you.

Another way of turning the subject without being too obvious about it is to nip in with 'That reminds me of ...' Again, this allows you to relate a story of your own. What your companion has been saying could remind you of a crisis, an amusing experience, a piece of wisdom that you picked up somewhere or a helpful snippet that you heard on the radio. It could be almost anything, as long as it is vaguely related to what you have been talking about. It's a gentle way for you to break the other person's flow, get a word in and, again, steer the conversation in a more interesting direction.

You don't need to talk all the time

It may happen that find yourself at a gathering where others present know each other well and want to talk about events or people you know nothing about; or haven't seen each other for a long time and want to catch up. It is only polite to let them carry on. Listen and learn, or perhaps listen and be entertained.

If you want to join in, don't try to change the subject; instead pick up on something they have been saying. If they've been gossiping, you could try enquiring, with a laugh in your voice, 'I have to ask – who are we talking about? She sounds awful.' This should remind the others that they ought to include you, and they'll probably have fun giving you the background to their relationship with this awful woman, whoever she may be. If the conversation is more serious, try something like 'I'm sorry, but I don't know much about the [person/issue] you're talking about. Could you fill me in?' Once you have the background, you can listen more intelligently, perhaps make a contribution and be part of the group when the conversation takes a different turn.

When all else fails

If it seems impossible to get away from a boring person – if there is no one to hand on whom you can fob him off, or if there is a waiter bringing drinks, so no excuse to make a dash to the bar – you may have to do something drastic. Even the most committed bores have to pause for breath sometime, so be prepared to pounce. Begin your interruption with 'That's fascinating, but …' and introduce the subject of your choice:

- 'That's fascinating, but did you see *Strictly* (or *Panorama* or *Match of the Day*) last night?'
- 'That's fascinating, but have you read *The Brothers Karamazov* (or

'Are you a Terry Pratchett fan' or 'Are you interested in manga')?'
- 'That's fascinating, but tell me – have you tried the Paleo diet?'

It really doesn't matter: in an ideal world your question will evoke an eager affirmative, but you're frankly past caring by this time. In fact, you're rather hoping that your interlocutor will say no, so that you can launch out on your own. Her Ladyship does not generally advocate hijacking a conversation in this way, but if negotiations have failed, direct action may be the only answer.

As an absolutely last resort, say, 'So nice to have met you' and move away. It isn't conversation, and it has to be carried off in a grand manner, but desperate situations call for desperate measures.

Too much information

We tend to assume that bores talk about only trainspotting or spreadsheets, but that is to ignore another archetype who can be every bit as difficult to deal with: the over-sharer.

In Her Ladyship's experience invalids and those who have recently been 'dumped' by a partner rank high on the list of those who assume that every passing stranger is interested in the most intimate aspects of their lives. She once overheard a customer in a newly opened local delicatessen giving the shop owner – and everyone else within earshot – details of her recent gall-bladder operation. From the rest of the conversation it was clear that the two women had never met before.

A friend of hers had a young colleague who had split up acrimoniously with a boyfriend and for several months could talk of nothing but his bad behaviour, her own misery, the general awfulness of men and the several mortifying one-night stands she had had in an effort to assuage her grief. Her Ladyship has no wish to be unsympathetic to anyone suffering from a broken heart; she merely feels that an open-plan office is perhaps not the best place for this sort of soul-baring.

Both of these, to her way of thinking, were severe cases of over-sharing.

While we can all be guilty of talking obsessively about ourselves when we have something on our minds, Her Ladyship's advice to those with this tendency is simple: be careful. Pour your heart out to a close friend or family member, by all means. But before you divulge personal information to someone you don't know well, take a moment to imagine how you would feel if you were on the receiving end of these confidences. Embarrassed? Uncomfortable? At a loss as to how to respond? A combination of the three? Then that is probably how the person you are talking to feels. Their position may be all the more awkward because they are sorry for you, don't want to snub you but don't feel able to help. You would also do well to ask yourself why they should even be willing to help: most people have enough going on in their lives, dealing with their own needs and those of their family and friends, without taking on the woes of a comparative stranger.

> **While we can all be guilty of talking obsessively about ourselves when we have something on our minds, Her Ladyship's advice to those with this tendency is simple: be careful.**

Remember, also, that because you don't know this person well, you don't know how discreet they are. They may turn out to be the local equivalent of a medieval town crier. Do you want to risk having your confidences repeated to all your mutual acquaintances? Particularly in a small community – be it a village or an office – news travels fast. You have to continue living or working there, uncomfortably aware that everyone knows about your ailing health, your romantic woes or your financial troubles.

Don't over-share online …

The above applies primarily to face-to-face encounters, but the advent of social media and online dating has made it all too easy to over-share not only with casual acquaintances but also with complete strangers. The Internet is full of horror stories about people who thought they had met their soulmate through a dating site, only to find that they were expected to become the third party in a previously undisclosed love triangle or had somehow given away financial details that had cost them their home and savings. For your own sake, Her Ladyship repeats, consider the consequences before you confide too freely.

Remember also that less can be more, even when it comes to sharing things you are deliriously happy about. You are not the only person who has the most beautiful baby/gorgeous new boyfriend/fabulous holiday in the world, and posting photos of any of these five times a day is going to irritate even the closest of your friends.

… or at work

It's all too easy to over-share in a business context, too, if you are nervous. An acquaintance of Her Ladyship's was once pitching an idea for a new piece of software. He had a good track record in his field; he had done his research and was confident that there was a market for his product; he had also tested it thoroughly and knew that it worked. All he needed was the money to take it to the next stage of development. Yet instead of explaining all these things to his potential backer, instead of coming across as authoritative, reliable and professional, he found himself babbling about his childhood, his ne'er-do-well father and his teenage experiences of shoplifting. Fortunately, the backer recognised a bad case of nerves when he saw it and gently but firmly steered the conversation back to the point. The deal was done, but it was a close-run thing.

I don't want to know

But what do you do if you are on the receiving end of this unwanted information? If you can make the excuse that you are busy, you have an escape route. In the delicatessen example given above, even if there are no other customers, you can make a show of slicing up meat, rearranging the display or disappearing into the back room to do some accounts. Similar evasive actions will present themselves if you happen to be in an office rather than in a food shop. 'Excuse me, I must get on' or 'The boss is breathing down my neck and I must get this finished' enables you either to leave the room or to put your head down and ignore any continuing chatter.

> **❝**
> **It's all too easy to over-share in a business context if you are nervous. Instead of coming across as authoritative and professional, you find yourself babbling. ❞**

But a social situation may be more tricky. The ploy for dealing with bores suggested earlier (dragging some unsuspecting person in to share the conversation) can work if the new arrival is someone the over-sharer doesn't know – you can only hope that they will be embarrassed at repeating intimate details in front of another stranger. It also gives you the opportunity to introduce a different subject. Say to the new arrival, 'Ali, this is Gemma. She works in the florist's on the market' (rather than 'She's just been telling me *all* about her daughter's bulimia'). Ali will naturally say something to Gemma about flowers, you can back her up and the two of you can steer Gemma on to a different course. Then, at a convenient break in the conversation, you can say, in a sympathetic aside, 'I'm really sorry about your daughter, but I'm not qualified to advise you. Have you thought about asking for professional help?'

Finding someone you know on the other side of the room can have the same effect. Say, 'I really need to talk to .... Come over and I'll introduce you.' If the over-sharer comes with you, you should again be able to change the subject; if they respond, 'No, thanks, I'm fine, don't let me keep you', take them at their word and make your escape. But do, perhaps, mention to the host that the person you have been talking to seems upset. Assuming they know your over-sharer better than you do, they may be better able to offer support and sympathy.

> **If the over-sharer says, 'I'm fine, don't let me keep you', take them at their word and make your escape.**

Strangers on a train (or plane)

The etiquette of talking to fellow travellers varies enormously according to where you live and how you travel. No Londoner talks to a stranger on the Underground – it's obviously against some by-law or other – but the bus or a bus queue is different. Idle conversations on a short journey are easy to strike up for the simple reason that they aren't important and aren't going to last long. If you find yourself next to someone chatty, you might find you pass an enjoyable few minutes; if you don't find them agreeable you can console yourself with the thought that one or other of you is getting off any moment now.

Commuters who routinely catch the same train and sit in the same carriage for an hour or so every day may start with brief nods of recognition, progress to idle remarks about the weather or the delays, and after a few months find themselves looking forward to the daily poker game on the way home.

Long-distance travellers often worry that they will get 'stuck' with a bore or a crank if they encourage the person sitting next to them to talk. On the other hand, you sometimes overhear people who were obviously strangers to each other at the start of the journey having interesting conversations. Does being too stand-offish mean you miss out?

It has to be your call, in Her Ladyship's view, and much depends on the length of the journey: she can think of few things worse than being talked at throughout a transatlantic flight. It makes sense, on any long trip, to be on friendly nodding terms with someone you are going to have to climb over every time you want to get out of your seat, but that doesn't mean you have to chat without a break for the entire journey. After all, the seven hours it takes to fly from London to New York (or the two and a half it takes to go by train from Glasgow to Manchester) may be the only time you have had in weeks to catch up on paperwork, or your last opportunity to polish the speech you are due to make when you get there. Even if you have no urgent work to do, it makes sense to arm yourself

> **66**
>
> **Idle conversations on a short journey are easy to strike up for the simple reason that they aren't important and aren't going to last long.**
>
> **99**

with a laptop, a book, a device on which to play games – anything that can make you look preoccupied. Then, if you encounter an inveterate talker, you can say something like 'I'm sorry, but I need to finish this before I get to Swindon' or 'I know it seems trivial, but I'm on level 7 and I'm in competition with my son.' If the other person keeps talking, answer with nothing more encouraging than 'Mmm' and they should soon get the message.

If they don't, try excusing yourself to stretch your legs. If nothing else, it will interrupt their outpourings. When you come back, make a point of opening your briefcase or laptop and getting on with something. Ignore any further attempts to attract your attention – at least until you have finished your work, or are near enough to the end of your journey that a few minutes' more chat won't hurt.

If you feel like talking, there are easy conversational approaches. Ask where your neighbour is going, if they have been there before and whether they are travelling for business or pleasure. Share your excitement at going to a new place, or joy at returning to a favourite one – if you are both heading for the same destination there must be

> **Does being too stand-offish mean you miss out?**

something you can talk about. Just be aware that if they start muttering 'Mmm' or retreat into their headphones, they may not be as eager to talk as you are.

The Art of Listening

The reason why so few persons are agreeable in conversation is that each thinks more of what he desires to say, than of what the others say, and that we make bad listeners when we want to speak.

La Rochefoucauld

"

The sad truth is that most of us are more interested in what we are going to say the moment we have the opportunity than in what our companion is saying right now. Her Ladyship is firmly of the opinion that you cannot be an interesting conversationalist unless you cultivate the art of listening. Try to resist the urge to drift off mentally when someone else is talking. Sooner or later all but the most committed talker will ask you what you think about whatever they are saying. It's always embarrassing to reply, 'Oh, I think compost is the answer' and then to be informed that they stopped talking about their rose bushes ten minutes ago and have moved on to their toddler's temper tantrums.

Learn to take a hint

People betray their interests and enthusiasms by the angle they take on a subject. The way they respond to a casual remark can give you guidance on how to pursue a conversation. Listen for clues.

If a remark about bad weather, for example, brings the observation, 'It's good for the garden', you can ask if the person is interested in gardening. The chances are they are, or they wouldn't have instinctively connected the rain with its effect on plants. If the same observation provokes a response about digging out winter clothes, they may be interested in talking about fabrics or fashion. If all the other person can find to say is that it is terribly dismal and makes them depressed, sympathise but try to find a bright side to remark on – perhaps that spring is just around the corner, or that you find the outlines of the trees in winter magical, or even that you plan to move to a Caribbean island when you win the lottery. As ever, you are trying to encourage the other person to have something enthusiastic and interesting to say. If you fail with the dismal person, you may just have to try being enthusiastic and interesting yourself, in the hope that something will rub off on your companion. Or fall back on the gentle moaning described in Chapter 3.

Sometimes the clues lie in what a person *isn't* saying. Learning to pick up on this is particularly useful in interviews and in buying/selling situations. If you are interviewing someone who is cagey about why they left their last job, make a note to check their references particularly carefully. If someone trying to sell you a washing machine emphasises its smooth lines and elegant appearance, you can be reasonably confident that it's not ecologically friendly or it's expensive to run or it doesn't actually get the laundry clean.

Other conversational triggers can emerge not just from what a person says, but from how they say it. This sort of thing can only ever be personal, but Her Ladyship is always intrigued by a person's choice of words: anyone may casually describe a politician as dishonest, for example, but someone who says that the same man is unscrupulous or deceitful or fraudulent has perhaps given the matter more thought. Acknowledging this, by saying, 'What an excellent choice of word – unscrupulous is exactly what he is' will show the speaker that you are listening attentively. Perhaps even better is, 'That's an intriguing word – why do you think he's fraudulent?', giving the other person the chance to elaborate.

> **Sometimes the clues lie in what a person *isn't* saying. Learning to pick up on this is particularly useful in interviews and in buying/selling situations.**

If words aren't your speciality, you can still pick up on a person's mood: 'I can tell you feel passionately about this' is a way of encouraging them to keep going – though it has to be said that if they are passionate about the subject they may not need much encouragement. If you want to steer them in a different direction, try, 'I can tell you feel passionately about this, but have you thought about how the French (or the neighbours or the board of governors) are likely to react?' Alternatively, you may notice their voice faltering or their eyes misting up, in which case you may choose to say, 'This obviously upsets you – are you sure you want to talk about it?' This approach is particularly appropriate if you have inadvertently introduced a sensitive subject or asked someone who has perhaps suffered a bereavement how they are coping. Very often such a person will say, 'No, no, I'm fine' and carry on; sometimes they will excuse themselves for a few minutes' respite – in which case you know it is time to change the subject when they come back.

Encourage the shy

There are some people who genuinely prefer to listen than to talk, and they are a godsend for those who are inclined to let their tongues run away with them. But there are others who would like to talk if only they had the nerve. It's easy for a shy person to be overwhelmed by even a small group: they may stand there smiling and nodding, but feeling unable to make a contribution. If you notice this happening, make a point of bringing them into the conversation. If the topic under discussion is a current news item, turn to the silent one and say, 'You're very quiet, Tom – what do you think?' If you and another member of the group have been talking about recent holidays, say, 'What about you, Tom? Have you been away lately?'

If Tom doesn't want to express an opinion or hasn't been on holiday, you have to be ready to gloss over the pause, perhaps by asking him another question that will encourage him to talk. But don't force it. If he doesn't respond to this sort of overture, you have to assume that he really is happier just listening.

" "

You're very quiet, Tom – what do you think about all this?

Oh, I don't know, I don't really read the papers.

Really? They're my great weekend treat. What do you do on Sunday mornings?

Well, nothing much, really. A few chores around the house.

Awkward silence. How much easier if Tom had had the confidence to say:

Oh, I don't know, I don't really read the papers. I normally listen to The Archers *on Sunday mornings and I can tell you anything you need to know about that.*

The conversation could then slide easily into favourite radio programmes, a subject on which Tom can presumably sparkle. And if you happen not to be an *Archers* fan, console yourself with the thought that you have managed to bring Tom out of himself, which was the object of the exercise.

" "

"

Dealing with interruptions

Interruptions happen. The phone may ring while you have friends round for supper. Someone may come up and say hello while you are talking to someone else. Someone may knock on the office door while you are in a meeting. It's nobody's fault, but the way you deal with the interruption colours how the rest of the conversation goes.

Answer the call, but keep it as brief as possible: 'I've got people here – can I call you tomorrow?' Introduce the new arrival and then turn back to the person who was speaking with 'I'm sorry, Charlie – do finish your story' or 'You'd got to the bit about the potholes.'

On the subject of phone interruptions, however, Her Ladyship prefers to leave the answering machine on and calls unanswered if she is entertaining, and she would certainly think it was very rude for a supper guest to answer a call on their mobile. She feels the same about people who answer the phone in restaurants. If, as a guest, you feel obliged to leave your phone turned on – because you genuinely need to complete a business deal, perhaps, or because you are anxious about an ill relative or a rampaging teenager – mention this to your host as soon as you arrive, making it clear that you wouldn't do it in normal circumstances but that this is a special case. If the call comes, excuse yourself and leave the room to answer it. Don't answer a call from anyone else, and once you have dealt with the important call, turn the phone off and put it away.

"

When is a conversation private?

There's listening and there's eavesdropping.

A friend of Her Ladyship's was having work done on her house. She chatted amiably with the builders both about the job and about this and that over coffee before they started work each morning. Then one lunchtime she overheard them discussing a film she had also seen recently. What was the etiquette here, she wondered. Was she entitled to join in the conversation – which was taking place on her own back doorstep – or should she respect the fact that this was the builders' 'down time' and leave them to talk in peace?

She opted for the latter and Her Ladyship is inclined to agree.

There are, however, occasions when butting in on conversations is a friendly thing to do. If you overhear someone wondering about how to get somewhere and you are able to give them directions, they are likely to be grateful. The people sitting next to you at a sporting event will probably be happy to include you in their conversation about the game (though you should, of course, maintain a discreet silence if they happen to be discussing a family crisis). In a coffee shop, you might hear two people talking about where they are

> **There are, however, occasions when butting in on conversations is a friendly thing to do.**

thinking of going on holiday, a show they are considering going to see or a restaurant they might try. If it happens to be a place you have been, a show you have seen or a restaurant where you have eaten, you can easily interpose, 'Excuse me, I couldn't help overhearing …' and express your opinion. Then take any further cues from the people you are interrupting. If they ask where you stayed, or whether the show was suitable for children, or if there was a reasonably priced set menu at lunchtime, they are obviously inviting you to carry on talking. If they say, 'Thank you very much' and turn back to each other, you can safely assume that they aren't interested in further contributions from you.

Taboo Subjects

Silence, therefore, and modesty are very advantageous qualities in conversation.

Michel de Montaigne

"

It has often been said that you should never talk about politics, religion, money or sex. Her Ladyship is inclined to think that a blanket ban on these subjects is a bit sweeping, but she would recommend that, before embarking on any of them, you have some idea of the views of the person you're talking to. It's all very well to make a disparaging remark about a politician to someone you know broadly shares your attitudes; it's not diplomatic to say the same thing to an unknown quantity who, for all you know, may be a card-carrying member of the party you are criticising. By all means ask a stranger his or her view on an issue of the day; just don't do it if you are a political activist or an insider. You're asking someone for their opinion, not giving yourself the opportunity to break into a rant.

That said, it would be a logical extrapolation to say that you shouldn't mention football in case, as an Arsenal supporter, you deeply offend a Chelsea fan; or express admiration of a Sondheim musical to someone whose taste may turn out to be for grand opera. There has to be a limit to the subjects to be avoided or conversation would founder altogether.

So, if you want to stray into an area that may cause a sensitive reaction, Her Ladyship's advice is to do it cautiously. Don't introduce the subject of football by ranting against Chelsea: say something like 'I don't

> **"**
> **If you want to stray into an area that may cause a sensitive reaction, Her Ladyship's advice is to do it cautiously. "**

know if you follow football at all. Did you see Arsenal versus Chelsea on Saturday?' Then, if the response is, 'Yes and, as a Chelsea fan, I have to say the referee was rubbish', you know where you are. By all means say, 'Well, I'm afraid I support Arsenal, so you can't expect me to agree with you', but say it lightly and with a smile. Then look for something positive you can say, a point on which the two of you might agree. You may find that you share a passionate dislike of any clubs based north of Watford; or that you can speculate harmoniously about England's chances in the next World Cup, or about the prospects of an up-and-coming player. A football conversation can now flow quite freely: you don't have to agree on every point, but because you began tactfully your disagreements should be more amicable than they would have been if you had charged in regardless.

'Delicate' subjects

Be careful about 'delicate' subjects too. Most people have a past: the stranger sitting next to you at dinner may recently have suffered a bereavement, serious illness, divorce, impoverishment or job loss that you know nothing about. Her Ladyship recently caught herself speaking

> **"** Whatever you do, don't persist with a subject that is causing anyone present embarrassment or distress. **"**

scathingly of someone in the news who was on to his third marriage, before remembering, mid-sentence, that the person she was talking to was twice divorced. Don't steam in, she now advises, before you have gauged the situation.

If you do commit this sort of gaffe, apologise – at once and only once. Making a fuss over your apology draws attention both to your tactlessness and to the other person's discomfort, and can only make matters worse. Then either change the subject or allow others to do so. 'I'm sorry, you must know much more about it than I do' or 'I'm sorry, I didn't realise, how horrid for you' throws the ball into the other person's court: they can then take it up or not, just as they choose.

Whatever you do, don't persist with a subject that is causing anyone present embarrassment or distress. If you are expressing an opinion on unemployment, for example, and your host points out that one of the other guests at the table has recently been made redundant, don't say, 'Oh I'm sorry, but it proves my point' or suggest that your new acquaintance is the exception that proves the rule. The moment you have moved from the general (your views on the whole issue) to the particular (a specific person's job loss), the atmosphere changes entirely and your having your say ceases to be important. What's more, if you fail to pick up on the fact that your host is discreetly trying to divert you, you risk offending him as well as the person who has lost his job. Quietly let the subject drop. If you really need to rant about unemployment, do so later to your partner, your taxi driver or the television newsreader next time it comes up.

Professional privacy

Other people are every bit as entitled to an evening off as you are. Don't ask a doctor whom you meet in a social situation for medical advice or a vet what to do about your cat's ear infection. In Her Ladyship's early days as an editor, she had a friend who worked for what was then the Inland Revenue. The two of them couldn't go anywhere, it seemed, without meeting someone who wanted to have a book published and someone else who wanted advice on their tax affairs. Her Ladyship has always been grateful she never had a close friend who was a chiropodist, a taxidermist or a funeral director.

As a side note to this subject, Her Ladyship is inclined to favour warning others in advance that one of their fellow guests has had an unpleasant experience. Saying – perhaps over the phone when the invitation is issued, or on the night, before the person in question arrives – 'In case it comes up, you should know that Ian lost his job recently' or 'Fran's mother died a few weeks ago' helps to avoid the sort of foot-in-mouth conversation just described.

Up close and personal

The conversational guideline that says, 'Ask them about themselves' is, as is so often the case, only a guideline. While not many people really hate talking about themselves at any price, some do, and even those who are normally quite outgoing may be touchy on some subjects. As mentioned above, someone who has just lost her job may be surprisingly sensitive to the question, 'What do you do?' If someone fobs you off when you ask an obvious question, accept the rebuff and talk about something else.

While 'How do you do?' is a formula requiring the answer 'How do you do?', 'How are you?' and 'Are you all right?' are genuine questions that could be answered in any number of ways. Be tactful about how you ask them of anyone who has been bereaved or has broken up with a partner; if they are *not* all right, they may want to tell you about it in private but not in public; or they may prefer not to talk about it at all. Following up with, 'You look really tired' or 'You look as if you've been crying' may be intended to be sympathetic, but may not be very comforting for the tired and stressed person who has just been indulging in a bout of tears in the bathroom. Keep your concern to yourself until the circumstances are right.

If the position is reversed and for some reason you don't want to answer an obvious question, try to prepare an answer, as discussed on pages 24–27. If you are caught unawares, evasiveness is your first line of defence. 'Well, that's a long story' should deter all but the most thick-skinned; if it doesn't, try 'I don't want to bore you' or even, 'No, really, it's too boring, let's talk about something else.' If you say this and then stop, you're likely to create an uncomfortable lull, so be prepared to leap in with a new subject: 'Tell me about your family' or 'Have you seen [latest much hyped film]/Have you been to [local beauty spot]?' It doesn't matter if it is a complete non sequitur, as you have made it clear that you want to change the subject. And giving the conversation a firm steer in a different direction makes it almost impossible for your conversational partner to revert to the troublesome topic.

> **“**
> **Giving the conversation a firm steer in a different direction makes it almost impossible for your conversational partner to revert to the troublesome topic. ”**

If the worst comes to the worst, reverse the embarrassment: give an overly frank answer. A friend of Her Ladyship's, living in a gossipy village and childless through choice, got so fed up of justifying her decision to comparative strangers that she took to telling people, in hushed and sorrowful tones, that she had been unable to have children. Word quickly got around and the impertinent questions dried up.

Before you persist in asking personal questions – even questions that didn't seem personal when you first asked them – spare a thought for the other person's embarrassment or beliefs. They may genuinely be unable to have children; they may be off alcohol because they are taking anti-depressants; they may be going caravanning close to home because they

" "

'*What would you like to drink?*'

'*Orange juice, thank you.*'

'*Are you sure you won't have a real drink?*'

'*No, thanks, orange juice is fine.*'

'*Go on, you'll make the rest of us feel guilty.*'

'*No, honestly, I've had a long week and if I have a glass of wine I'll fall asleep halfway through dinner.*'

'*Oh, surely just one won't hurt.*'

Have you reached screaming point?

" "

can't afford to go abroad. Think how you would feel if you had to admit any of these things to a new acquaintance, and hold back.

In the same vein, don't assume everyone is like you. These same people may not *like* children or alcohol or travelling. It's their privilege.

Asking what seem like harmless questions may turn out to be uncomfortable; so may imparting apparently innocuous information about yourself. As with any subject, you introduce it because it is interesting to you and in the hope that the other person will be interested too. Be sensitive to their response and don't harp on about something that clearly doesn't inspire them or is for some reason causing them distress. Tread gently, for example, when embarking on a tale that shows a member of your family in a bad light. Being dismissive or rude about your nearest and dearest may be funny to those who know them well (and know how much you love them really) but can be embarrassing to someone who takes you seriously and is surprised that you want to share such intimate details with them. Similarly, a paean of praise of your talented five-year-old may be upsetting to someone struggling with a child who is anything but perfect.

White lies

'At least I'm honest' is the frequent cry of those who are renowned for putting their foot in it, trying to capture the moral high ground while the structure of society crumbles around them. In Her Ladyship's view the moral high ground is by no means always where such people belong – whoever first said, 'Honesty is the best policy' had clearly never been asked, 'Does my bum look big in this?'

In social conversation, there are many times when economy with the truth – a white lie – will make things flow more smoothly. In the changing room of a clothes shop it is perfectly acceptable – indeed, it

> **"**
> **In social conversation, there are many times when economy with the truth – a white lie – will make things flow more smoothly.**
> **"**

is kind and supportive – to tell a friend that the dress she is trying on does nothing for her (thought you might not phrase it exactly like that). Once she has bought it and is wearing it to a party, you should keep that opinion to yourself.

White lies can also take the form of polite mumbling: unless you are prepared to sustain a serious debate, and the circumstances in which you find yourself make this appropriate, it may be better not to take issue with a stranger's political opinions, or with their views on health foods or complementary medicine. For all you know, their aging mother may have been evicted from her home thanks to a change in landlord/tenant legislation or had a long struggle against cancer that was alleviated by a form of treatment that you consider mumbo-jumbo. Tread warily until you can be sure that what to you is no more than an entertainingly forceful exchange of views is not a deeply personal and potentially hurtful matter to your antagonist.

When Her Ladyship says 'The circumstances make it appropriate', she means that, once it has been established that the topic of conversation is not painful to one of those involved, she has no objection to a heated discussion between two or three people standing in a group. Their differences of opinion, as long as they don't become loud and abusive, will affect no one else. But she recommends you not to inflict this sort of altercation on a dinner table, where it will prevent other people from carrying on separate conversations, and may cause embarrassment to those who would rather not have fierce debate over the chocolate mousse.

On the other hand ...

If the person you are speaking to is truly obnoxious, you may be justified in feeling that keeping quiet and letting them carry on is going to ruin your evening. In a party situation you can just walk away, having discovered an urgent need for the loo, the bar or a breath of air; or you can take drastic action as described on page 74.

But what if you are stuck next to someone unpleasant at a dinner table and face having to sit next to them for another two hours? You have a number of options:

- to grit your teeth and bear it
- to force the person to be quiet
- to change the subject
- to bring someone else into the conversation to lighten your load
- to turn away from them and talk to someone else.

Assuming that quietly gritting your teeth is not what you want to do, say firmly to someone whose opinions you find offensive, 'Shall we agree to differ? And talk about something else?' Before you say this, make

> **"**
> **If the person you are speaking to is truly obnoxious, you may be justified in feeling that keeping quiet and letting them carry on is going to ruin your evening.**
> **"**

sure that you have another subject prepared, so that you can continue without a break, 'Did you see the Rembrandt exhibition at the National Gallery?/Are you going to the local fête next week?/Where did you get that handsome tiepin?'

If you need something a little stronger and are prepared to have a heated discussion, try 'I can't agree with you there', then turn to someone else at the table and say, 'Sam, back me up here. This gentleman is saying XXX and I think YYY.' Assuming Sam shares your views on the subject (and you shouldn't use this approach if you aren't confident that she does), the two of you should be able to beat your neighbour into some form of submission.

But very often a heated discussion is precisely what you would prefer to avoid. If you really don't want to continue the subject, say, 'I can't agree with you and I wouldn't like to spoil Julie's party by having a row', turn to the person on your other side or opposite you and start talking briskly about something else. Give your objectionable neighbour as little chance as possible to interrupt until you are happy that the conversation has been steered into safer waters.

Right Place, Right Time

The true spirit of conversation consists in building on another man's observation, not overturning it.

Edward Bulwer-Lytton

"

From first dates to funerals, special occasions don't happen often enough for many of us to take them in our stride. This chapter deals with some of those circumstances when it is more important – and more difficult – than ever not to say the wrong thing.

Weddings and civil partnerships

The Finns have a charming habit that Her Ladyship would love to see more widely adopted. They produce a 'wedding directory' – a booklet containing a brief paragraph of background information on every guest, written by the bride and groom or someone else closely involved. Each table setting includes a copy, so that guests have the opportunity to glance at their neighbour's name card and look them up before embarking on conversation. This enables them to begin by remarking, 'I see you're a history teacher' or 'I see you're keen on classic cars' rather than asking 'How do you know X & Y?' or the more bluntly phrased 'So who are you, then?'

Weddings can be awkward occasions for many guests, but whatever your reason for feeling a bit left out, the normal guidelines for conversation apply.

In the absence of such an aid, weddings can be awkward occasions for many guests. You may be the only one of the bride's schoolfriends with whom she has kept in touch and therefore know no one outside the bridal party. Or you could be the partner of a relation or an old friend, invited because the two of you go hand-in-hand. Whatever your reason for feeling a bit left out, the normal guidelines for conversation apply: if you're circulating, find someone who looks congenial and is not already engrossed; introduce yourself and try to discover what you have in common. If you're sitting next to someone, ask what their connection is to the bride and groom and see where you go from there.

Remember that this is supposed to be a happy occasion, so be particularly careful about treading on other people's toes. Her Ladyship frankly does not recommend following the line adopted by an elderly character in the film *Four Weddings and a Funeral*, who asked a young woman if she was a lesbian simply because she had admitted to being unmarried. The elderly lady felt that it was more interesting than saying, 'Oh dear, never met the right chap, eh?' In Her Ladyship's view, this is one occasion when it might have been better to err on the side of dullness.

Weddings can be particularly difficult for the single or the recently widowed. Don't make disparaging remarks about the pitfalls of wedlock unless you are sure you aren't talking to someone who is longing to find them out or is missing them desperately.

Christenings and other naming ceremonies

Much the same applies as for weddings. If you happen to hate babies but are present under sufferance because you are this one's uncle and there was a three-line whip in the family, keep your views to yourself unless you are certain you are talking to a kindred spirit.

Funerals and memorial services

'Did you know him/her well?' is a useful starting point here, provided you don't ask the question of a member of the deceased's close family. But this should be an easy gaffe to avoid: even if you don't know the family, you should be able to identify them. They will normally sit in the front row(s) during the ceremony, some of them may give readings or make addresses, and afterwards they are unlikely to be standing around on their own waiting for someone to talk to them.

Over the refreshments that are often served after the ceremony, there is no need to stick to mournful topics of conversation. As always, try to gauge the mood: a funeral for someone who has died prematurely will be very different from that of an elderly person who lived a rich and happy life. But don't assume that everyone feels the same way you do: you may think the occasion is a celebration of a life well lived, but the surviving partner or children may be inconsolably sad.

Reminiscences about the deceased often lead to laughter and to the feeling that 'it was a great party – he would have loved it.' Even so, Her Ladyship advises against telling jokes (as opposed to anecdotes), calling out to someone at another table or generally becoming riotous. It's a funeral, not an excuse for bacchanalian excess, however enjoyable it may turn out to be.

Whatever the apparent mood, a funeral or memorial is likely to be an ordeal for those who were close to the deceased. Some get through the day by joking and laughing; others may be subdued and talking only to be polite. Take the tone of your conversation from them: be light-hearted if they are light-hearted, sombre if they prefer to be sombre. It's often difficult to find words to express your condolences, but your presence on these occasions is more important than what you say. A simple 'I'm so sorry' is much, much better than nothing. Pressing someone's hand is an affectionate way of expressing

> **Whatever the apparent mood, a funeral or memorial is likely to be an ordeal for those who were close to the deceased; take the tone of your conversation from them.**

sympathy and may be preferable to hugging someone who looks as if they will burst into tears at any moment. You may not be embarrassed by their weeping in public, but they will be, so try to avoid being the cause.

Particularly in a large gathering, it may be tactful to leave without saying goodbye. If the widow or children of the deceased are engrossed in conversation when you want to leave, don't interrupt them. Slip away quietly and telephone a few days later to offer support and tell them they are in your thoughts.

Hospital visits

The difficulty here is that a person who is confined to a hospital bed is unlikely to have done anything much recently. Their conversation is all too often restricted to their ailments and the vagaries or unpleasant habits of the person in the next bed. If the illness is a long one and you are visiting every day, you may feel that the conversation (or at least the interesting part of it) is very one-sided and you may well run out of things to say.

Tell yourself, first of all, that this is not about you. Your visits are to support and if possible cheer up the patient. Begin each one by asking how they are feeling and, if applicable, what the doctor had to say, what news there is of their condition and the possibility of their going home. Ask if there is anything practical you can do: the simplest things may seem overwhelmingly important to someone who isn't well. Imagine being in hospital during a hot summer, for example, and finding it impossible to persuade the busy staff to bring you as much water as you wanted to drink. A visitor armed with a bottle of Perrier would be welcomed with disproportionate gratitude.

> **Tell yourself, first of all, that this is not about you. Your visits are to support and if possible cheer up the patient.**

Once the obvious subjects are exhausted, it is up to you to sustain a conversation. Come prepared with an anecdote or two about what has happened since your last visit. This may be irksome if your last visit was only this morning, but remember that you have been outside the hospital ward – you have seen more of the world than the patient has. Describe an incident at work, what your children have been up to, something funny that happened in the supermarket. Mention something upbeat that has been in the news – a celebrity baby or the Oscars, perhaps; it is probably best to avoid rail crashes, terrorist outrages or proposed public spending cuts. Try to be cheerful and positive: a person who is bedridden doesn't want to listen to you moaning about the heavy traffic you had to endure in order to visit.

Try also to bring the other person into the conversation, encouraging them to reminisce (something the elderly in particular love to do) or to remember a shared experience. Even the flowers in the hospital garden could remind you of a visit you once made together to another garden. There doesn't need to be a very marked resemblance: the point is to trigger a happy memory and stimulate the patient to talk about it. Even if you have to do the reminiscing and intersperse your commentary with 'Do you remember?', you may find the patient smiling at the memory.

Be sensitive, however, to the patient's mood and state of health. If they are elderly or seriously ill, they may not be able to talk for very long at a time. Hospital visitors are often disconcerted by the person they thought was eager to see them dozing off mid-sentence: if this happens, go and find the coffee machine and come back 15 minutes later – you may find that a little nap has restored the patient's energy. If they don't feel up to talking, they may like you to read to them from the newspaper, a magazine, a novel or a favourite poem. Or they may derive comfort just from knowing that you are there, perhaps holding their hand. Not all conversation has to be verbal.

Talking to children

This is not a parenting manual and Her Ladyship wouldn't dream of giving advice to anyone about dealing with their own children. But many childless people find it difficult to talk to children, and even parents may struggle to chat to children other than their own.

The first thing to remember is that children don't care about conversational rules. They won't engage with you just to be polite, nor is the average nine-year-old interested in your concerns, your views on the government's foreign policy or how outraged you are that the bakery in the town centre has closed down. You have to talk about something that is of interest to them – which may mean letting them do most of the talking in the conversation.

With small children it's easier to communicate and make eye contact if you bend or crouch down so that you are nearer their height. Then ask them 'open' questions – the kind that can't be answered by 'yes' or 'no'. This is even more important with children than with adults: an adult will recognise that the question 'Is that your car?' is an invitation to talk about the vehicle's performance, safety features and audio system. Ask a child, 'Is that your cat?' and you could well receive a one-word answer, because they haven't learned to extrapolate in the same way. 'Tell me about your cat' is much more likely to produce an enthusiastic response.

Try not to be thrown by make-believe. If you ask a child to tell you about his pet and he claims to have a dragon in the back garden, go along with it. Ask what colour the dragon is, what it eats and if it needs to be taken for long walks.

> **Ask children 'open' questions – the kind that can't be answered by 'yes' or 'no'.**

Most children will enjoy telling you you are being silly: dragons don't go for walks, you may well be told triumphantly, because they can fly.

Even when a small child is being factual, you may find yourself out of your depth, because his perceptions revolve around his own little world. Ask what class he is in and you won't be told 'Year One' or 'Grade One'. It's much more likely to be 'Ms Blakeney's class' and you'll be expected to know who Ms Blakeney is. And don't waste your time with questions about dates, times and numbers. Although they will probably know that they are precisely four and three-quarters years old, asking, 'How old do you think I am?' may produce any answer between 16 and 92 – both unimaginably ancient if you're aged four and three-quarters.

Try not to show frustration if you can't make sense of a story a child tells you. You'll probably find that narrative drive gets lost amidst a lot of apparently irrelevant detail. It doesn't matter. Throw in the odd question to encourage the child to continue, but don't try to pin her down on matters of fact or logic. You'll spoil everything. And don't expect to understand the rules of a game as explained by a six-year-old. She's likely to start in the middle, explain technicalities that make no sense to the uninitiated and leave out such trivial matters as 'What's the object of the game?' or 'How do you know who's won?' If you're going to play, try to get a parent or elder sibling to give you a whispered rundown while the child is getting the counters out of the box, or logging into the game on her iPad.

Talking to teenagers

Parents of teenagers who are routinely either monosyllabic or rude at home are sometimes amazed to be told by a neighbour, 'It's always such a pleasure to have Stephen come round. He's so polite and friendly.' 'Oh?' they're tempted to reply, feeling not a flicker of recognition for this description of their son. 'Stephen who?'

Many a parent would suggest that the only way to talk to teenagers is to leave them alone for seven years and come back when they are in a better mood. But again Her Ladyship is not addressing parents here, and her advice is to remember that you have an enormous advantage when talking to teenagers: you are *not* one of their parents. They'll probably rather like you if only for that reason.

> **Talk to teenagers as if they were adults: ask what they have been doing and what they are interested in.**

Teenagers are on the way to being adults and will object to being patronised. Talk to them, therefore, as if they were adults: ask what they have been doing and what they are interested in. If the answer is 'Nothing much', try something more specific: what sort of music they like, if they are following a current sporting event, what plans they have for the holidays. Express interest if you can; ask for clarification if they name a band or a style of music that means nothing to you. Who knows, they may find they enjoy telling you about their enthusiasms and you may enjoy listening to them. Contrary to rumours circulated by parents, not all teenagers are grumpy, unsociable philistines.

Other age differences

It's natural in any gathering, whether business or pleasure, to gravitate towards someone of about your own age. But sometimes – particularly in a business context – you're obliged to deal with people who belong to a different generation.

Say you are attending a fund-raising dinner or an artist's private view. In the former case you may be acting as host on a table of, perhaps, ten people of varying ages; in the latter you may be meeting, greeting

> **66**
>
> **Cultivating a sense of detachment really helps to reduce the embarrassment you feel about accosting strangers.**
>
> **99**

and encouraging visitors old enough to be your parents to circulate (and buy the art). Or you may be a guest being hosted by someone young enough to be your son or daughter. Her Ladyship's advice in such a situation is to take a step back from yourself. Tell yourself that, for the duration of this evening, you are not you, the private individual who finds this sort of event nerve-racking. You are the marketing manager for your company, the representative of an important client, the potential purchaser of a painting. It is not yourself that you are pushing forward, it is the professional person who is paid to do this job or who is seeking information about a possible investment. Cultivating this sense of detachment really does help reduce the embarrassment you feel about accosting strangers.

Be aware, also, that you are probably no more uncomfortable than the older or younger person who doesn't know what to say to you. And in a business-related social context such as the examples just described, you automatically have something in common: the reason you are there. As host, you should know who the people on your table or your guest list are (because you have done your homework) and make an effort to make them feel welcome. 'You're Antony (or 'You're from XXX & Co.); I've heard a lot about you – great to meet you at last' is a good start. 'How nice of you to come. Have you been interested in XXX's work for long?' or 'What's your connection with the charity?' are other useful openers. If, as host, you find that one of your guests doesn't know much about the work or the charity (or whatever it may be), say, 'Let me tell you a little more about it' and enlighten them. Again, you will be able to do this, Her Ladyship says firmly, *because you have done your homework*.

Age-difference problems aren't confined to the workplace, of course. The average 20-year-old may well find it hard to know what to say to an elderly grandmother, not realising that someone born 50 years before the mobile phone was invented may be baffled by talk of Twitter and Instagram. That old lady may well, however, have a fund of memory and anecdote of a time long before her grandchild was thought of, and it can be accessed by simple questions along the lines of 'What was it like when you were my age?' or 'What did you do before you had iPhones?' Contrary to rumours circulated by the young, 'old' isn't necessarily synonymous with 'boring'.

Meeting the neighbours

If you were brought up on 1960s American sitcoms, you may think the best way of greeting new neighbours is to turn up with a freshly baked cherry pie, but in Her Ladyship's experience this is probably even more inconvenient than appearing on the doorstep with a bottle of wine before the newcomers have had time to unpack the corkscrew and the glasses. Far better, in her view, is to tap on the door or accost them in the driveway and suggest they come for coffee or a glass of wine later.

Not every newly moved-in neighbour will want to come out on their first night; they may be too busy settling in or too exhausted to be sociable, so have another date to offer them (the day after tomorrow, perhaps, or next weekend) if they turn down the original invitation. If they turn that down too, don't push it. Say something like 'Well, we'll do it sometime. We'll be seeing each other around' and leave them for a little while.

If you are the new arrival(s) and do want to meet your neighbours, it's not difficult to find an excuse to knock on their door: asking for help or advice ('Can you lend me an electric drill? Mine's in a crate somewhere but I have no idea where' or 'Can you recommend a plumber? I don't want the washing machine leaking all over the floor and it will if I try to plumb it in myself') is a good way of breaking the ice. Then you can make sure you invite them in for a drink – as soon as you have found the corkscrew and the glasses.

Dating conversation

First dates are always nerve-racking, whether you are a teenager going on one for the first time or a recently divorced 50-something back in circulation after a lapse of some decades. Even if you have met your date several times before (at work, perhaps, or as a friend of a friend), there's an awkwardness about the possibility of moving your relationship onto another level; if you've met online and have now decided to meet in the flesh, there is the greater worry that the other person will change their mind the moment they set eyes on you.

Nobody is likely to be at their conversational best in this situation, but it may be comforting to remember that the other person is probably as nervous as you are. Even if they are talking a lot and seem very confident, it could be their way of covering up their anxiety.

What to talk about – and what not to

Assuming that you haven't taken one look at your date and decided that this is all a terrible mistake, you want to appear at your best: friendly, interesting and prepared to be interested in him or her. So, the first priority is not to put them off.

- If you are looking for a serious relationship, keep quiet about it in the early stages (certainly on the first date and probably on the second and third too). If you have met through a dating site you have probably specified that you are interested in what Her Ladyship believes is known as an LTR, but even so it is potentially frightening to become too intense too quickly.

- On the other hand, there's no need to insist that you are interested only in a casual fling, whether or not this happens to be true. That may be how you think you feel, but why spoil your chances of getting to like someone, out of bed as well as in?

- Even if you both know that you are both divorced, don't talk endlessly about your former partner. It will give the other person the impression that the ex still plays an important part in your life; what you want to convey is that you are ready and willing to move on. Even more importantly, if you are widowed, don't overplay the virtues of your deceased spouse. No one finds it easy to compete with a ghost.

- By all means mention your children – you don't want their existence to come as an unpleasant surprise to someone who thought you were footloose. But don't go on about their activities and achievements unless you are genuinely encouraged to do so. Specifically, don't talk about the problems you are having with your disgruntled teenagers: unless your companion has difficult teenagers of his or her own and you can swop light-hearted horror stories, that comes firmly under the heading of Too Much Information on a first date.

66

> **As with most conversation, you want to draw the other person out, find out more about them and discover what you have in common.**

99

- Feel free to talk about your job, especially if it is an absorbing one, but don't mention your salary. Once you've told someone you are a hedge-fund manager or a social worker, they'll be able to draw their own conclusions about your position on the financial ladder – and at this early stage it isn't any of their business, anyway. If you feel inclined to see each other again (and possibly again and again), the question of what you can and can't afford to do together will become relevant, but for the moment don't brag about your yacht or make a virtue out of buying clothes from charity shops.

It isn't all about conversation

It takes some of the pressure off a first date if you go somewhere you don't have to talk all the time. If you're sitting opposite each other in a bar or a restaurant, there's not much to do except eat, drink and talk. But if you go to a sporting event, an exhibition, a funfair or even for a walk in the park, you can fill in gaps in the conversation by talking about what you are seeing and doing, and you'll be less uncomfortable in those moments when you feel you have nothing to say.

So what do you talk about? As with most conversation, you want to draw the other person out, find out more about them and discover what you have in common. Start by expanding on what you already know: 'You were telling me about your walking holiday' or 'X [the person who introduced you] says you were brought up in Italy. Whereabouts?' This shows that you have been paying attention (always an attractive quality), as well as encouraging the other person to shine by talking about their own experiences and enthusiasms. After your companion has regaled you with her youthful experiences in Italy, it should be natural for her to ask you about your own childhood. If yours was spent in a characterless suburb or dull one-horse town, try to find something to enthuse or be comical about. Saying, 'Mine was very boring compared to yours. We never went anywhere more exciting than the Isle of Wight' will sound self-pitying unless you can follow it with, 'There was a really grumpy landlady who hated my brother playing the guitar in our room' or 'I remember once we were in a caravan and it rained solidly for a week. The people next door had a Labrador puppy and it kept sneaking into our caravan and making muddy marks all over the beds. Mum had a fit.'

This raises all sorts of possibilities: your Italian-raised companion could start talking about dogs, or about how house-proud her own mother is, or about the fact that it does rain in Italy too, you know, and counter with an anecdote of her own. One way or another, your conversation is up and running.

Speed-dating

There's surely no occasion when first impressions are more important than when you have only a few minutes to 'make your number' with someone. You want to stand out from the crowd without seeming weird.

For once, it's not only safe, it's actually advisable to dispense with the banalities. It has been recorded (Her Ladyship is not sure how) that two-thirds of speed-daters start by asking 'What do you do for work?'; most of the rest, trying to be interesting, go for 'What do you do for fun?' Somebody who has already answered this question 15 times is not going to sparkle when it is asked by speed-date number 16. Instead, try asking a hypothetical question as a way of gauging your date's personality and tastes: 'If you could go anywhere in the world to a concert of your choice, where would you go and who would you hear?' This presupposes that you are interested in travel and in music; if not, you could try the same sort of question about a fantasy meal or sporting event. Her Ladyship recommends avoiding whimsical questions of the 'If you were a flower/ animal/colour, what would you be?' type: with only four minutes at your disposal, you don't want to waste precious time while your date ponders whether she is turquoise or *eau de nil*, nor to risk her writing you off as a pretentious anorak.

When Body Language Isn't There to Help

'Then you should say what you mean.'
'I do; at least – at least I mean what I say –
that's the same thing, you know.'
'Not the same thing a bit!'

Lewis Carroll

Increasingly, in this hi-tech age of instant and constant communication, 'conversations' don't take place face to face; many of them don't even involve talking. All the more important, then, to make sure the words say what you want them to say in the tone you mean to use.

On the phone

It has been said – by those who first espoused texting and social media – that the telephone is an extraordinarily impolite instrument. Its loud interruption of meals, work or other activities, its screech of 'Talk to me now, talk to me now' are, if you want to look at it that way, just plain rude.

So whether you are phoning a close friend, your mother or an unknown sales 'prospect', you should always ask if it is convenient for the other person to talk. You are not going to have a cosy chat, never mind make a sale, if you are speaking to someone who has half an eye on the children, the television news or the fact that they have a meeting in ten minutes.

If you are on the receiving end of a call and it is not convenient, say so. 'I'm just putting the kids to bed/sitting down to watch David Attenborough/trying to finish this report before I pack up for the day' are perfectly legitimate responses to someone who has called out of the blue. Offer to ring back later in the day, the following evening or even, if you are very busy, next week.

As the caller, always be friendly to a secretary, colleague, partner or housemate who answers the phone: their attitude to you colours the way they pass your message on (or indeed whether or not they bother to pass it on at all). Barking, 'Tell her to call me' when told that someone is in a meeting, and putting down the phone without a word of thanks or farewell, is not going to get anyone on your side. The PA who tells her boss that 'a brusque man from XXX' called is not doing you the favours she might do for 'that charming man from XXX'.

On the telephone, of course, words and tone of voice are everything. Strangely enough, smiling while you talk will make your voice sound warmer – you'll probably find that you do it without thinking if you are talking to someone you are fond of or on a subject you are enthusiastic about, but it's worth making a conscious effort if you are making a sales call or trying to get the other person to do you a favour. On the other hand, nodding or shaking your head is a waste of energy unless you are on Skype or FaceTime.

> **On the telephone, of course, words and tone of voice are everything.**

If the other person is frowning or surreptitiously carrying on with the crossword in the hope that you will go away soon, something of their lack of attention will also filter its way through to the other end of the line. This should tell you that the conversation is reaching a natural close. Even during a casual catch-up with close friends or relations there seem to be pauses when you are both thinking about what to say next, because you've said what you needed to say and frankly there isn't much else for the time being. Companionable silence may be very pleasant between partners reading the papers on a Sunday morning, but it is hopeless on the telephone. And awkward silence is even worse.

> **In Her Ladyship's view, it is the height of rudeness to keep someone talking after they have expressed a desire to stop.**

Learn to end a conversation gracefully. There are any number of explanations you can give for wanting to hang up, as long as you phrase them politely and express some regret at 'having' to go: 'I'm really sorry' can be followed by 'I have to get on with my paperwork/feed the cat before she tears the place apart/ finish icing Hugh's birthday cake', or anything else that is appropriate to your circumstances and the time of day. You can always add something like 'I'll talk to you later in the week' or '… before you go on holiday'. If the other person doesn't take the hint, you may have to be a bit firmer: 'I really have to go.' In Her Ladyship's view, it is the height of rudeness to keep someone talking after they have expressed a desire to stop. This is particularly true if you initiated the call and the other person is trying to bring it to a close: even if they assured you you weren't interrupting anything, they may have meant that they had 20 minutes to spare, not an hour and a half.

Online conversations

Not even tone of voice can help you here. Make sure you mean what you say, say what you mean and don't say anything that could be misinterpreted as sarcastic, angry or dismissive. And don't hide behind the distance that electronic media provide: never email, text or post anything that you wouldn't say to the person's face.

Nor should you send messages when you are angry, upset or the slightest bit inebriated. Particularly on social media, anything that you write is out there, in the ether and beyond your control, forever more. Think carefully before you post anything that may be embarrassing the next day/next year/if a prospective employer, your mother or a possible new boyfriend or girlfriend looks at it. Some people refuse to be friends with their parents (or indeed their children) on Facebook to avoid feeling the need to censor their own posts, but Her Ladyship is inclined to think that not posting anything censorable in the first place is a better option.

Tempting though it may be to dash off a searing, blistering, heart-broken reply to someone who has upset you, it is always better to sleep on it. If you draft something to make yourself feel better in the heat of the moment, can you be absolutely certain that you are going to press 'save' rather than 'send'? Some programs nowadays have an 'unsend' function: if you send something by mistake, you can get it back, but you have to do it within a few seconds, which means you have to be sufficiently au fait with your email system to be able to undo the damage before, in fact, the damage is done. In Her Ladyship's experience, this is unlikely to be the case if you are sending a maudlin late-night message to an ex. Her advice is not to risk it.

Beware predictive text

In Her Ladyship's view, too many modern devices think they know better than you do what you want to say. For some reason we are less inclined to check instant messages than we once were with handwritten or typed letters. Put these two factors together and you can produce undesirable results. A female friend of Her Ladyship's once texted a male colleague a message that was supposed to be about a cab; predictive text decided (somehow) that it was about a bed. As the message contained the suggestion of sharing, this caused considerable embarrassment to one party and amusement to the other. (It also, as an aside to the main issue here, promoted a discussion in the woman's office about the insidious way Americanisms have invaded British English – 'It wouldn't have happened if you'd said "taxi",' one pedantic colleague pointed out.)

> **Always proofread your messages before sending them.**

Her Ladyship also recently received a text from a friend who travels a great deal in the course of her work. After apologising for having to reschedule their forthcoming date, she ended it, rather tersely 'Oz'. Her Ladyship, assuming that this meant her friend had to go to Australia, replied appropriately but, as it turned out, mystifyingly. The friend, whose name is Polly, had intended to sign her message 'Px'. Predictive text had decided differently.

The moral? Proofread your message before sending it. Accidentally writing incomprehensible nonsense to a friend may be no more than a brief waste of time for both of you; in a business context, if you offer to share beds when you mean cabs (or taxis), it can be tricky to put your relationship back on an appropriate footing.

Words at Work

*My idea of hell on earth is a literary party
and I have an uneasy feeling that this post
carries with it a lot of sherry-drill with
important people.*

**Philip Larkin, on refusing the
post of Professor of Poetry at Oxford**

"

M uch of the talking that occurs in and around the workplace may not really justify the description of 'conversation' – or necessarily include sherry-drill – but it is still a form of communication that involves give and take. It also, perhaps more than any purely social conversation, requires us to consider the other person's needs and wishes.

Situations such as interviews, presentations and sales pitches force us to tread a fine line between making the best of ourselves and bragging. Her Ladyship was once present at what was meant to be a brainstorming session, with everyone on an equal footing: the important thing was to come up with ideas, not to impose any sort of hierarchy. The meeting was spoiled by a newcomer to the group who entirely hogged the conversation. He boasted of his previous achievements, dropped the names of influential clients and, by trying to make himself sound like the

> **"**
>
> **Situations such as interviews, presentations and sales pitches force us to tread a fine line between making the best of ourselves and bragging.**
>
> **"**

most creative thinker since Leonardo da Vinci, made himself obnoxious. Yes, of course, he wanted to establish his credentials, but he left no room for others to contribute.

As with the anxious over-sharer described on page 78, the result was a waste of time for people who didn't have time to waste, and the potential loss of business or a job opportunity for the person who had got the tone of the conversation wrong.

Let us in both these cases give the culprits the benefit of the doubt and say that their problem was nerves. (We may be being overgenerous, but never mind.) Like so many other difficulties with conversation, these can largely be overcome by planning. Prepare yourself by considering what you have to offer that the people you are meeting want. Answers might include: your experience, your expertise in a particular field, a way of improving a certain aspect of their operation, a product that can make life easier for them.

What do they not care about? How cleverly you pulled off a recent deal, how much you know about something that is not on the agenda, how many famous people you have dealt with. And they absolutely don't want you to drown out what other people have to say and turn an informal exchange of ideas into a keynote speech.

Before the meeting starts

There's often a certain amount of hanging around before a meeting starts, usually waiting for the boss to turn up. Colleagues can take this in their stride and talk about anything from the latest sales figures to last night's *Dragons' Den*, just as they would over the coffee maker or in idle moments in each other's offices. But if you are an outsider – a salesperson making a pitch, perhaps, or an auditor wanting to discuss the latest accounts – you have to be more careful.

First of all, be discreet. By all means introduce yourself to anyone you don't know and join in harmless conversation, but if office gossip is going on around you, ignore it. Second, don't start pitching your wares until everyone is sitting down and ready. It is highly likely that the most important person in your audience – the decision-maker – is the one you are waiting for, so you will have to go through it all again and risk boring the people you have spoken to already. In addition, Murphy's Law dictates that you will be interrupted as soon as you reach a key point, meaning that you lose your momentum and the point seems less impressive when you come back to it. Better, perhaps, to say hello to the early arrivals but then to retire to look over your notes, double-check your figures and generally keep your distance.

Presentations

Before you start preparing a presentation, establish what this particular audience wants to know: the speech that went down so well last time may not be remotely relevant to today's group. Ask the person who has invited you to speak what they are expecting of you (in terms of length as well as of content) and tailor your remarks accordingly.

Even if you are doing a formal presentation, be prepared to be interrupted with comments or questions. However carefully you may have tried to suit your talk to their requirements, the people you are addressing are the only judges of what is and is not relevant to them, so try not to be perturbed if they drag you away from your script. They haven't read your script, so they don't care if you miss a bit: if that bit is indispensable to the message you want to convey, draw them back again once the diversion has been dealt with. Otherwise, let it go. They'll be more impressed that you answered their questions than that you worked your way meticulously through every item in your PowerPoint.

Remember, also, that they have probably come to listen to you either from choice or because they feel they might learn something. To a large extent they are on your side: they *want* you to be interesting. You don't have to win them over: you simply have not to let them down.

Interviews

Because what you talk about at interviews obviously depends on the nature and level of the job concerned, Her Ladyship's advice can only be generic. That said, there are a number of general principles that will stand you in good stead whether you are hoping to become CEO or post-room assistant. Many of them come, yet again, under the heading of 'Be prepared'.

- Before your interview (ideally before you fill in the application form), find out as much as you can about the company ethos as well as what it does. Most companies' websites have an 'About Us' page that includes something about their principles, their attitude to their staff, suppliers and customers, and to the environment. They'll be portraying themselves in the best possible light, of course, but it can still be useful to find out what image they are trying to promote and where they say their priorities lie. Check their social media pages, too. Pick up on key concepts such as 'sustainability', 'corporate responsibility', 'innovation' and work these words into your conversation, to show that you care about the same things as they do.

- On the other hand, avoid mindless jargon of the 'thinking outside the box' and 'worst-case scenario' type. If you rely on these clichés, your interviewer may get the impression that you don't have an original idea in your head.

- Give some thought to why you want this job rather than any other. How does it fit in with your long-term plans? (Even if it doesn't, be careful not to suggest that you would be using the post as a stepping stone towards better things.) Be prepared to elaborate on what you feel you can do for this company – and sound excited about it. Ask intelligent questions: something like 'I noticed on your website that …. Can you tell me a bit more about that?' will indicate that you have had the gumption to read the site.

- You are almost certain to be asked about your previous experience. Don't be panicked by the thought that you don't have any: of course you do. Even if you are applying for your first ever job, you haven't just emerged from the womb. Think about what you are good at and what you've achieved in the past: perhaps voluntary work or responsibilities at college have given you valuable knowledge or insights. Single out something that indicates you are good at working as part of a team if that is what the job requires; or emphasise something that shows you are imaginative and creative, or determined and capable of seeing things through to the bitter end. Many job descriptions use the word 'self-starter': they mean someone who isn't going to sit around waiting for others to tell them what to do. If you are going to claim that that's you, be prepared to back it up.

- Give some thought to what you do in your spare time and how that might be relevant to your prospective employer: a love of sport may indicate that you are a team player or, if you prefer an individual sport such as squash, that you are competitive. Either could be a useful attribute, depending on the nature of the job. A passion for travel may show that you have an open mind and are curious about other cultures (useful if you are applying for a post in a multinational company); if your interests are more domestic, they could demonstrate that you are reliable and conscientious, which could be particularly attractive to an employer looking for commitment. Call it spin if you like, but Her Ladyship would prefer to describe it as presenting yourself to the best advantage.

> **If you are going to make a claim about yourself, your skills or your experience, be prepared to back it up with examples.**

- You may also be confronted by questions that aren't specifically about the job or your qualifications. Being asked 'Tell me about yourself', 'What sort of person would you say you are?' or 'What did you learn from your last job?' may floor you if you haven't thought about it in advance. If you are asked something you're not prepared for, try to say something positive like 'That's a good question' rather than 'Um', 'Er' or (worst of all) 'I don't know.'

- Bear in mind, too, that not all interviewers are good at interviewing. You may find that you have done all this preparation and they are not asking the right questions, not giving you a chance to shine. If that happens, look for a way of working positive information about yourself into the conversation. Treat a closed question as if it were an open one: if you're asked, for example, if you are prepared to work overtime at short notice, don't just say, 'Yes.' Back it up with the anecdote you have prepared to illustrate your flexible approach.

And a few things not to say

Going back to that all-important first impression, make it a priority to arrive on time. If you think that's unlikely (because traffic is going to be bad or you aren't 100 per cent sure where you are going), aim to arrive at least 15 minutes early. Then if your journey goes smoothly you have time to have a cup of coffee and to assemble your thoughts; if it doesn't, you still shouldn't turn up too frazzled. If you are going to an unfamiliar area, it may be worth doing a 'dry run' a day or two before, so that you know how far it is from the station or can identify an unnumbered building on an industrial estate.

However – and to revert to the subject of conversation – if by any chance you are late, apologise as briefly as you can and let the interview move on. You have already wasted some of your interviewer's time, and a lengthy description of the stressful experience you have just had risks making them write you off as a hysteric. If your train was delayed, they may wonder why you didn't phone to warn them: if the answer is that you couldn't find your phone or didn't have their number, Her Ladyship ventures to suggest that you are not presenting the most competent aspect of your personality.

Don't ask about salary, holiday entitlement, flexitime or promotion prospects too openly or too soon. However cunningly you disguise it, the question 'What's in it for me?' is off-putting to an interviewer – you want to convey that you are able and willing to give rather than to take. You've

probably put current salary or salary expectations on your application
form, anyway: they wouldn't be interviewing you if you were going to
demand thousands more than they wanted to offer.

And remember that, however wacky and imaginative the company
you are hoping to enter may be, you are not there yet. You are in an
interview, which by definition requires a certain amount of formality. Just
as you aren't dressed in torn-off jeans and a skull-adorned goth tee-shirt
(and Her Ladyship devoutly hopes she didn't need to mention that), so
you shouldn't be lured by the interviewer's youthfulness and friendly
manner into describing that embarrassing incident after a few drinks
last Friday night or the fact that you were up at four o'clock changing the
baby's nappies.

Group exercises

Not all interviews are one-on-one. Recruitment for the graduate training
scheme of a large company may involve group exercises: you may be
asked to work with other applicants to analyse a business strategy, for
example, or discuss a way forward from a hypothetical crisis.

In this situation, the company is interested not so much in your
capacity to do a specific job as in personal attributes, such as your
ability to work in a team, your communication skills and aptitude for
problem solving. It's likely to be looking for someone who contributes
but doesn't dominate; who has bright ideas but is flexible enough to
listen to what others have to say; and who can perhaps take someone
else's suggestions and develop or improve on them. Here are a few
pointers on what and what not to say and do:

- Just as in any other conversation, listen to yourself and stop if you
  realise that you are talking too much, boasting or wandering from
  the point.

- Don't put anyone else down. Even if you think their ideas are
  hopeless, find a tactful way of saying so. Saying something like

'That's interesting, but I wonder if we should be a bit more assertive/cautious/creative' acknowledges the contribution and introduces your own views modestly. Have a suggestion at your fingertips before you start dismissing the other person's: 'I wonder if we should be a bit more assertive: how about an advertising campaign in the run-up to the summer holidays?'

- Be pleasant to everyone from start to finish. You may end up working with them and that won't be easy if they have you down as a smart alec or a bully. As with all first impressions, you may struggle to make them change their minds.

- Stay focused on the task in hand. Even if you haven't been given a time limit, you will in part be judged on your ability to concentrate and to produce results. Don't let the conversation drift off into last night's TV or the weekend's weather prospects. There'll be time for that during the tea break.

Is it work or is it play?

Communications experts lay particular emphasis on 'weak links' when it comes to succeeding in business. By this they don't mean the weak links that are likely to make a chain break. They're contrasting casual acquaintances, vague contacts, friends of friends of friends, with the 'strong links' of family, friends and close associates – people you see all the time and who you know will help you if you need them to. The importance of the weak link is serendipity: that stranger you chat to at a conference may make a passing reference to a person it might be worth your while contacting or to a business opportunity you might be interested in; you follow it up and, hey presto, it changes your life.

Life-changing encounters don't come along that often in Her Ladyship's experience, but the point is that random snippets of information crop up in conversation in a way that simply doesn't happen when you email or phone someone about something specific. So do bright ideas that weren't on the agenda for the meeting, but that popped into someone's brain in the course of conversation afterwards. Even in our technophiliac twenty-first century, there is no substitute for the face-to-face encounter, and – once you are away from strict agendas and time limits – for allowing what you talk about to move just a little off-piste.

Business lunches

There are some professions in which much business is done over lunch. To those who don't work in publishing, advertising, marketing or the like, this may seem the ultimate in self-indulgence; but to the inexperienced negotiator who knows that a deal may be won or lost over a Caesar salad or sole Véronique, the business lunch can be nerve-racking. Discussing

> **66**
>
> **Her Ladyship is firmly of the opinion
> that a bit of small talk has
> to precede the business part
> of the lunch.**
>
> **99**

business isn't the problem – the anxiety occurs over when you should start doing it, and what you talk about before that.

If you are the host

Her Ladyship is firmly of the opinion that a bit of small talk has to precede the business part of the lunch. As host, you should arrive a little before the appointed time so that you are there to greet your guest. You can then ask harmless but courteous questions about his (or her) journey, whether or not he knows this restaurant or, if he comes from another city, whether or not he knows this part of the world. If a waiter doesn't appear promptly to do this for you, offer your guest a drink. Once menus have been brought, and unless for some reason you are lunching in a restaurant of your guest's choice, you can express opinions about

> **66**
>
> **If your memory is unreliable, you might even choose to make notes after each lunch of any personal details you feel you would like to 'remember' for next time.**
>
> **99**

the food, along the lines of 'The spaghetti carbonara is particularly good here' or 'The portions are very generous – the steak and kidney pie is excellent if you're hungry.'

Prepared hosts will already have established if their guest has any preference as to cuisine, and won't be taking a vegetarian to a restaurant famous for its carvery. They'll also have chosen somewhere that is within their own or their company's budget and should make it clear that their guest is welcome to have anything they choose. It does happen, however, that your guest has expressed a desire to go to a certain restaurant and you find yourself somewhere that is more expensive than you intended. Remarking casually, 'I think I'll stick to the set menu, but do go for the à la carte if you prefer' will encourage most people to say, 'No, no, the set menu looks fine.' Similarly, the well-mannered guest won't insist on a bottle of Château Margaux if the host is sticking to mineral water – though if you do this too ostentatiously you run the risk of looking mean. Better, perhaps, if keeping your guest sweet is important, to slacken the reins on the expense account just this once and resolve to be very restrained for the rest of the month.

If you have met the person before but don't know them well, it is a good idea to prepare yourself by searching your memory for something they have told you about themselves. Then you can ask, 'Weren't you about to go to Berlin last time we met? Did you enjoy it?' or 'Did you sort out that problem with your son's school? Has he settled in?' This not only gives you something to talk about while the general messing about of ordering is being done; it shows that you care enough about this person (and the business they may put your way) to have paid attention to what they have said to you. If your memory is unreliable, you might even choose to make notes after each lunch of any personal details you feel you would like to 'remember' for next time.

Only once the ordering has been done should you introduce the subject of business, and even then you should keep it general for the time being. Saying something like 'I was reading about your new Australian branch on your website: is it up and running?' shows that you have done some research and are intending to have a serious conversation, but isn't so intense that your companion can't enjoy his food.

> **66** **You can generally tell from your guest's demeanour whether or not he is eager to get down to business straight away and act accordingly. 99**

Then there comes the moment when you have to get to the point. Some say it shouldn't happen until the main course has been removed and pudding or coffee ordered; others feel that midway through the main course is more appropriate. You can generally tell from your guest's demeanour whether or not he is eager to get down to business straight away and act accordingly.

If you have a list you want to discuss, make sure it is tailored to the individual you are dealing with. Lunch is not the place for complicated and lengthy presentations, but rather an opportunity to become better acquainted with a client or prospective business partner and perhaps to brainstorm a little about ideas that might work for both of you. Don't waste people's time, in other words: they'll be less keen to do business with you if you do. And don't ask them important questions when they have their mouth full.

Once you have launched yourself into business talk, it is difficult to return to trivialities: don't attempt this unless your guest does. Offer more coffee or another drink and, if your guest seems to be in no hurry, let him take the conversational initiative. Just beware of any attempt to pump you for confidential information or gossip. Remember the advice Her Ladyship gave in Chapter 4 – if you don't know someone well, you don't know how trustworthy they are. Telling a slightly indiscreet story may give your guest the comfortable feeling that you are confiding in them, but if you choose to do this be careful not to mention sums of money or anything else that really should be kept private. However keen you may be to form a bond with your companion and put them at their ease, there is a risk – whether you are host or guest and especially if the wine is flowing – of moving into dangerous territory: dangerous because you may not know much about your companion's private life, political views or other such matters and you could inadvertently cause offence; or because you find out too late that the other person is more adept at industrial espionage than you are.

In an ideal world, it will be obvious to both of you when it is time to wind up your conversation: if your guest shows signs of lingering and you need to go, say so tactfully: 'Well, do you think we've talked about everything? Shall I get the bill? I'll email you this afternoon to summarise what we've agreed' or 'I'm really sorry, I have another appointment. But this has been most productive. Thank you.' Then make sure you do the follow-up email or send the material you have promised promptly.

If you are the guest

If you are the guest at a business lunch, you have presumably been invited for a reason and can, if you choose, take the conversational lead from your host. On the other hand, if you aren't sure you want to do business with him – or don't know what he wants from you – it is up to you to cut through small talk and ask. Don't try to initiate business conversation until you have ordered and can concentrate, but once that is done it is perfectly reasonable to say, 'So how can I help you?' or 'What did you want to talk to me about?' However much your host may want to soften you up with chat and good food, you may have a meeting at 2.30 and need to get on with it. Business lunches are a balancing act for all concerned.

Business conferences

Conferences are a strange combination of work and socialising, with the potential pitfalls of the office party (see page 140) thrown in. Much of Her Ladyship's advice about talking discreetly (see page 77) applies to conferences, with the proviso that, outside the conference room itself, these are ideal places for networking. If you get to know someone in a similar line of business socially, you are more likely to feel that you can pick their brains, ask for their support or share information once you are both back in the office. They are also more likely to reciprocate. This doesn't, of course, mean that – either at the conference or in the future – you should share confidential financial or HR information, but you might pit your combined wits against a powerful but difficult customer or the problems of seasonal peaks and troughs.

> **Much of Her Ladyship's advice about talking discreetly applies to conferences, with the proviso that, outside the conference room itself, these are ideal places for networking.**

Introducing yourself to strangers at a conference is, in Her Ladyship's experience, rendered much easier by the fact that they are likely to be wearing name tags that also give the name of their company. You may realise that you have had dealings with this person but never met them face to face: in that case, you have the beginnings of a relationship already and should grasp the opportunity to build on it. If not – assuming it is a conference for people from the same industry – you have probably at least heard of their company and can find something to say about it. And if that isn't the case, be candid: 'I'm afraid I don't know your firm. What do you do exactly?' Provided they aren't the market leaders, they should have no reason to take offence and should be happy to promote themselves to you: that is, after all, part of the reason they are there. You can then ask any questions that seem appropriate, provide the same sort of information about your own firm and – assuming you find this person congenial – be relieved that you have someone you can chat to in the next break.

If by any chance you don't find them congenial (and in Her Ladyship's experience every conference provides at least one crashing bore), excuse yourself on the grounds that you have just spotted someone you simply must talk to or that you want to write up your notes while everything is still fresh in your mind. Leave the room if necessary, reappear a decent interval later and try the same approach with someone else.

Most conferences involve formal sessions with speakers, which gives you another topic of conversation over coffee afterwards: you can approach almost anyone and ask what they thought. As with the general advice about party conversation given earlier, however, check who you are talking to before you make any negative criticism: make sure it isn't the speaker's colleague or spouse, or the conference organiser who booked her. If you do want to be critical, you can still be tactful: 'Not really my field' is an acceptable way of expressing disappointment; 'Complete bloody waste of time' is not.

As for the socialising that often follows the formal sessions of a conference, Her Ladyship's advice is to be wary of too much alcohol and the indiscretions – professional or personal – that can easily follow. You may be away from home and from your day-to-day colleagues, but the people you are with are still part of the same industry, and you can bet your life that, when it comes to gossip, it turns out to be a smaller world than you could ever have imagined. Don't tell yourself that, as the theatrical profession puts it, 'What happens on location stays on location'. It doesn't.

Office parties

Her Ladyship is not sure if there is research to back up this assertion, but in her opinion more indiscretions are committed at office parties – and more hungover remorse suffered as a result – than on any other occasion. The sad truth is that, at an office party as at a conference, you are to a certain extent still at work. The person you are talking to may be an amiable drunk this evening, but on Monday morning he or she will still be your boss or a member of your department. Bear that in mind before you drink too much, pay compliments that could be interpreted as sexist or complain vociferously about the lack of Christmas bonus. Office parties are not the occasion to tackle anyone about your salary review, the ridiculous restrictions against checking Facebook on your work computer or any of the other items on your painstakingly compiled list of what is wrong with the company.

Instead, talk about same things you might on any other social occasion – family, hobbies, that wide range of apparently random subjects mentioned in Chapter 3 – while avoiding anything too personal. Bear in mind the advice on over-sharing given on page 77. In these circumstances, your boss, other senior people in the company and members of other departments that you don't know very well should be treated as the comparative strangers in whom it is unwise to confide too much.

That said, like business lunches and conferences, office parties are a balancing act. Her Ladyship's caveats notwithstanding, they are an opportunity to get to know members of other departments and perhaps overturn any barriers there may be between you. If you often communicate with a certain colleague by email, make a point of

> **"**
> **Like business lunches and conferences, office parties are a balancing act between behaving with discretion and embracing the opportunity to get to know other colleagues.**
> **"**

seeking that person out and saying how nice it is to meet them at last. As a conversational opener you can ask if they have sorted out a particular problem or give them an update on a project of mutual concern. You probably won't turn into Gavin and Stacey, but this face-to-face contact may enhance your working relationship and make the other person more inclined to help you out in the future. Plus it may be enjoyable. Which is, as Her Ladyship hopes this book has shown, what conversation is all about.

Ten Golden Rules

To sum up, Her Ladyship would like to offer the following as her 'top ten tips'. If you take nothing else away from this book, try to remember these:

1. *Don't turn conversation into the enemy.* It should be stimulating, informative and enjoyable, not a test for which you are awarded marks out of ten.

2. *Be prepared.* Whether you are going to a friend's party, a business conference or a charity dinner, do some homework. Be ready to answer basic questions about yourself – and to make yourself sound interesting.

3. *Practise, practise, practise.* Get in the habit of talking to strangers, on the bus or in shops, in museums or at the gym. You may be amazed at how many amiable people there are out there.

4. *Don't despise small talk.* The point of asking 'Have you come far?' is not to find out if the other person has come far, it's to encourage them to tell you about themselves. The more you learn about them, the more likely you are to discover something you have in common.

5. *Don't be a bore.* If you see people's eyes glazing over, stop droning on and ask your companions something about themselves. Even better, try to be sensitive enough to stop talking before this happens.

6. **Don't share intimate details of your life with people you don't know well.** On the one hand, you will probably embarrass them. On the other, you don't know if they are to be trusted with a confidence, so you run the risk of having your private affairs spread around the neighbourhood or the office.

7. **Gauge the situation and the mood before you express strong opinions.** You don't want to offend strangers, particularly if they are friends of your host, by laying down the law on subjects on which they hold strong opinions that happen to clash with yours. Be sensitive, too, to individual circumstances – what may seem a harmless remark about the unemployment figures may appear callous and hurtful to someone who has recently lost their job.

8. **Be cheerful at weddings, christenings and other similar occasions.** Even if you are a hardened cynic who doesn't believe in connubial bliss and who can't find a good word to say about babies, keep your views to yourself and congratulate the newly-weds or new parents with enthusiasm.

9. **Behave appropriately at funerals and memorials.** Take your tone from the bereaved and be sombre if they choose to be sombre. Even if the occasion is a 'celebration of the life', don't let yourself become raucous.

10. **Remember that conferences and office parties are still 'work'.** Beware the indiscretions that too easily result from conviviality: don't leak confidential information to a new best friend who may turn out to be a business rival.

99

A Final Word

Conversation. What is it? A mystery! It's the art of never seeming bored, of touching everything with interest, of pleasing with trifles, of being fascinating with nothing at all.

Guy de Maupassant

When Her Ladyship had almost completed this book, she was approached in the street near her home by a man she had never seen before.

'Excuse me,' he said, in the manner of someone who was going to ask the way to the post office.

Her Ladyship stopped, prepared to be helpful.

Then he observed, 'You obviously like pink.'

Her Ladyship was indeed wearing pink. She replied, 'Yes, I do, I love pink.'

The man said nothing else. Not 'It suits you' or 'I hate it' or 'It's a cheerful colour' or anything else at all. He simply nodded in a friendly way and walked on.

Was this a conversation? Not really. Did it count as 'practising talking to strangers', as discussed in Chapter 2? Probably not. But it made Her Ladyship laugh; it made several of her friends laugh when she told them about it; and it prompted conversations about 'other strange encounters we have had in the street'. It would no more appear on a list of recommended topics of conversation than the idea of going up in a rocket and viewing the Earth from space. But it does suggest that, if you have an open mind about conversation, you can find it – and enjoy it – wherever you go.

146

Acknowledgements

Her Ladyship is, as always, grateful to everyone who supplied suggestions, experiences and anecdotes to help with this book. This time that includes Airdre, Carol, Elaine, Geoff, Heather and Dylan, Jill, Niki, Rebecca, Ros, Rosey, Raj and the party in Anglesey, and the man in Rochester Row who may or may not have liked pink.

References

Blyth, Catherine *The Art of Conversation* (John Murray, 2008).

Caplin, James *I Hate Presentations* (John Wiley, 2008).

Fox, Kate *Watching the English: The Hidden Rules of English Behaviour* (Hodder & Stoughton, 2004).
  This wonderful book is the source of the expression 'shared moaning' mentioned on page 58, though some of what Kate Fox says about moaning is inspired by Jeremy Paxman's *The English* (Michael Joseph, 1998). She is also the source of the quote about 'drifting' into conversation, given on page 52.

Koch, Richard, & Greg Lockwood *Superconnect* (Little, Brown, 2011).
  This is where the advice on weak links given on page 133 comes from.

Lowndes, Leil *How to Talk to Anyone* (Thorsons, 1999).
  Leil Lowndes is the expert who offers the advice on greeting a stranger as an old friend given on page 19.

Mather, Diana **Secrets of Confident Communicators** (Hodder & Stoughton, 2014).

Morgan, John Debrett's *New Guide to Etiquette and Modern Manners* (Headline, 1996).

Not Actual Size, *The Art of Being Middle Class* (Constable & Robinson, 2012).

Powell, John *Why Am I Afraid to Tell You Who I Am?* (Argus, 1969).

Powell was the 'five levels of communication' philosopher mentioned on pages 53–54.

Taggart, Caroline *How to Greet the Queen* (Pavilion, 2014).

Lady Troubridge *The Book of Etiquette* (Cedar Books, 1958; first published 1926).

Wallace, Danny *Awkward Situations for Men* (Ebury Press, 2010).

The quotation on page 70 is from Anthony Quinn, *The Streets* (Jonathan Cape, 2012).

I have also drawn inspiration and information from these websites:

www.businessballs.com/body-language.htm#body-language-introduction

www.businessinsider.com/8-things-to-always-say-in-an-interview-2013-5?IR=T

career-advice.monster.com/job-interview/interview-questions/best-things-say-in-interview/article.aspx

www.pickuplinesgalore.com/speed-dating/

www.psychologytoday.com/blog/sideways-view/201412/the-secrets-eye-contact-revealed

www.realsimple.com/work-life/work-life-etiquette/oversharing

io9.com/scientific-studies-explain-the-best-ways-to-talk-to-chi-582531307

www.stevenaitchison.co.uk/blog/6-ways-to-dramatically-improve-your-eye-contact-skills/

www.speeddater.co.uk/sd-news/hi_speed_daters

www.telegraph.co.uk/lifestyle/stella-magazine/

targetjobs.co.uk/careers-advice/assessment-centres/275425-group-exercises-what-to-expect

Index